Country Library

FISHERMAN'S FOLLY

BB writes for all those anglers who relish the solitude of summer days spent at the water's edge. He conjures up the joys of sunlit watermeads and midge-haunted pools, the bronze and silver beauty of the fish and the excitement of the waiting and the battle, in words which stir the heart of all those who love fishing. This book says something of how big fish may be caught and of the places where he has angled for them; he describes what manner of birds, beasts and wild things he has met with in his solitary vigils (surely Thorney Pool must be the Paradise of which all anglers dream); and we share his thoughts on such tranquil occasions.

In 1949 a book appeared under the title of *Be Quiet and Go A-Angling*. Its author, Michael Traherne, was none other than BB. After its post-war appearance it dropped from view, but BB has now chosen to draw on it as the basis of this new book, so that it may now be enjoyed by the many people who have delighted in his books down the years.

He invariably ended his warbling song with a sweet
musical refrain which was particularly pleasing

FISHERMAN'S FOLLY

'BB'

Illustrated by
D. J. Watkins-Pitchford

THE BOYDELL PRESS

© 1987 D. J. Watkins-Pitchford

First published 1987 by The Boydell Press
an imprint of Boydell and Brewer Ltd
PO Box 9, Woodbridge, Suffolk IP12 3DF

ISBN 0 85115 249 X

British Library Cataloguing in Publication Data
'BB'
  Fisherman's folly.—(Country library).
  1. Fishing—Great Britain
  Rn: Denys James Watkins-Pitchford I. Title
  II. Series
  799.1'2'0941   SH605

ISBN 0 85115-249-X

Printed in Great Britain by
St Edmundsbury Press, Bury St Edmunds, Suffolk

The artifice of fishing is displayed not only in the delusion of the fish, but to some extent in the delusion of the fisher also. Let him but have the power of persuading himself that the boy in him has never grown up, or better, let it be so without his knowing it, and the world is his oyster.

HUGH SHERINGHAM, *Coarse Fishing*

CONTENTS

Introduction viii

I	The Summer Fisherman	1
II	Thorney Pond	8
III	Night Fishing at Thorney Pond	20
IV	The Fisherman and his Weapons	36
V	Float, Hook, Line and Sinker	42
VI	Fishermen All	47
VII	Harper's Brook	51
VIII	An Idle Interlude	55
IX	The Temple Pool	64
X	Shreds and Patches	72
XI	Restless Rods	78
XII	The Untouchable	89
XIII	Shadows and Reflections	97
XIV	A Mixed Bag	107
XV	In the God's Good Time	114

INTRODUCTION

If you are a purist, a scorner of float and worm, if you look for instruction on how to fish, and where, this is not the book for you.

This might be described as a rambling discourse on fishing in general and of carp fishing in particular, for the author has had many a magic midnight hour in search of this species, especially the big fellows for nowadays a big carp can outweigh a salmon.

Some regard fishing as a foolish sport, hence the title, yet there are few rogues amongst true fishermen, they are peaceable fellows, addicted to strong ale (in moderation) and with a deep and intense love of the peace and quiet of the countryside whether by pond or stream.

I have tried to convey this in my book, it is the very essence of fishing that I am after.

I am a shooting man. I have enjoyed my days with a gun, especially wildfowling, but those are restless days compared to those I have enjoyed by some remote park pool or gliding river.

Fishermen may sometimes be foolish if untruthful, but we are not fools.

'BB'

CHAPTER I

THE SUMMER FISHERMAN

Fishing is, on the whole, a summer sport, just as shooting is a winter one. True, I have met anglers who pursue their craft all through the year, a hardy race who will even go forth when ice is on the water and snow upon the banks. But to me, a summer fisherman, the idea of setting out with a rod on a frosty morning seems slightly indecent.

All the same, I must confess I am lost in admiration when I see a man, well muffled and overcoated, live-baiting for pike or roach-fishing, on a January morning. He is of a more hardy stock than he who spins for pike or fly fishes for grayling. The latter can keep on the move, he can have change of scene, he is not anchored to one place, hunched on a seat-basket, a trembling drop striving to freeze on the tip of his nose. Your winter float-fisher is a man in whom the hunting instinct is very strong, he is akin to the Eskimo waiting by an ice hole, he should live in an igloo.

I always maintain that to get full enjoyment out of fishing you must possess, in a certain measure, the hunting instinct. This applies to shooting-men as well. The eating of your fish should be the sublime termination of the whole business.

This view, however, is purely personal: probably ninety per cent of anglers would disagree.

I know very many who obtain complete enjoyment out of fishing and who have no interest whatever in the catch once it is on the bank. This to me is inexplicable. I would go further and say that to me such angling is pointless: one might just as well chase a golf ball or play Bridge.

The passion for fishing usually begins in boyhood. I doubt whether there are very many who have taken it up late in life and become ardent enthusiasts, and later I shall describe my early apprenticeship to the sport.

Another point: one does not often find a man who is an 'all-rounder'. By that I mean, it is rarely one meets with a man who takes as keen delight in watching a float as in casting a fly. Men like Arthur Ransome and the late Hugh Sheringham come into the 'all-rounder' class. To get the most out of fishing you should belong to this order.

Of course, the fly-fisher looks down on the coarse-fisher. The sight of a worm impaled on a hook is a shocking spectacle to the purist. The coarse-fisher does not despise the fly-fisher; he only wonders at his waste of effort. He will maintain that you can catch as many fish, if not more, by simply sitting still. Indeed, the idea of any movement at all is distasteful to him. He knows by experience that fish are sensitive to vibration, and thinks that it really is quite remarkable that the fly-fishers manage to catch anything at all! He regards them as restless souls who have not the true inner spirit of the Brotherhood. Quietness, immobility, is the watchword, not stumbling along the river bed with the arm and rod continually belabouring the fish as with a whip.

This is because the float-fisher haunts still waters and slow-moving rivers, he has the wariness and caution of the heron and kingfisher, he has the same patience, a reflective turn of mind.

I have watched herons competing with me beside still waters, and often wonder if they are not philosophical birds. The greatest appeal which coarse-fishing has for me is the utter peace and harmony of one's surroundings; it is a lovely lazy life. Though you are watching your float there is time to look about you, to let the peace of this green world lap you round. It is the most delicious form of idling known to me.

I know no other sport, save wild-fowling, in which you can withdraw from the workaday world so successfully, where all worries can be forgotten, where Nature can hold you so mesmerised, so entranced. I am sure that the heron feels this in his own way as he stands among the green sedges hour after hour. Mind you, I am the last to believe that animals and birds feel and reason in a way that is comparable with our own. That is utter nonsense – one only has to read the second-rate 'animal' stories to realise how false it is. Henry Williamson's *Tarka the Otter* rings true from beginning to end. Tarka does not think of life as we do, his awareness is in the passing second. That is why a child lives so vividly. As W. H. Hudson says in one of his books, children are only little animals; they are closer to life than we are; we can learn much from them.

When I say I think that herons are philosophical birds, I mean that I believe they get a vast measure of enjoyment out of their solitary life. The wheeling ripples from a questing moorhen which breaks up the reflection of the overhanging willow, the low summer hum of insects in the tree tops, the motionless globes of the yellow water-lilies – all these must surely give them a measure of delight. The heron, however, does not wonder at the restless martins and swallows which sweep to and fro over the pool in quest of flies; it does not think that they would be far better off if they were to stand with steadfast patience beside the water's edge; it does not regard them in the way the coarse fisherman regards the fly-fisherman. I compare the coarse-fisherman to the heron because they have something in common: this love of the quiet cool places they share together. Fly-fishermen are mere wagtails by comparison, though the wagtail's life can be just as jolly; as I know for myself, for I am both a fly- and coarse-fisherman, though by no means skilful at either.

Yet for that I have said, I do not believe that the heron, when it is standing waiting for a fish, is always thinking of its belly any more than the coarse-fisherman is. But if there should be the slightest hint of a fleeting shadow, of the slow cautious approach of a feeding fish, then that fierce round eye becomes a trifle more wide open, its intense burning fire more bright.

Perhaps – who knows – its heart beats faster, just as mine does on such occasions. The non-fisherman may laugh when I say that there have been times, while I have been waiting for a big fish to come along, when my heart has raced at an

I know of no other sport, save wildfowling, in which you can withdraw from the workaday world so successfully.

alarming rate. To sit quite still without a movement, with the heart hammering away nineteen-to-the-dozen, is quite an experience. The fly-fisher has some outlet for his nervous excitement. When he sees a good trout rise under a bush, he can begin his stealthy advance, he can move his legs and arms.

Even your Test fisherman, stalking his trout from behind the cover of the meadowsweet, can move his limbs.

I am no admirer of the cat, but I consider that the cat has the right mental equipment for a coarse-fisherman; indeed some cats are extremely good fisher-cats – I have met several in my pilgrimage through life. The cat waiting for the mouse, the heron for the fish, the man watching his float, all have a common bond. I believe that the cat in the ditch, crouching among the ground ivy, takes delight in his surroundings as the heron does, and that he does not think of his belly until his half-shut eye notes a slight stir among the leaves. We can learn much from the cat.

Restless spirits passing along the bankside must often wonder at us as we sit motionless. They must often remark at our folly; they ask each other what it is that makes a fellow man act so strangely, and they perhaps speculate (as I do about the heron) on what is passing through the angler's mind.

After all, what *do* we think about when we are waiting for a bite? In my own case I am not aware that I am thinking of anything in particular; I am just letting the peace and beauty of my surroundings sink into the very core of my being, as an animal basks in the warmth of the sun.

Very frequently, if I am angling for tench or carp, I ponder on the ways of these fish, their habits and their form. I have been a fisherman for so long now that I can at times, in complete quietness and serenity, sense when a big fish is approaching my bait. It is a curious experience, a sort of sixth sense manifesting itself.

Laugh, laugh, you scoffers, you restless unhappy mortals with town minds who do not know peace beside the quiet waters, but it is true!

There may be no movement among the weeds, no ripple on the pond, no sound of any sort; but I know that down below in the sub-aqueous world a shadowy bulk is looming ever nearer with imperceptible movements of its fins. Out of the fog of water there draws near a glowing ruby-orange eye as the bronze tench comes close. I see with my inner vision the puff, slow puff, of thick lips, the swivelling of that lidless gaze upon the pink and sheeny lob worm, well scoured and lively, which crawls, a captive of the impaling hook, before his very nose.

It is no surprise when the scarlet quill, which for so long has been resting quietly, a perching place for dragonflies, begins to quiver oh, so slightly...

There are few things in the realm of sport which stir me so profoundly as that first curtsey of a float. It seems to nod reassuringly, as much as to say, 'I told you so, patient man-on-the-bank – here we go!' (I get the same kind of thrill when I see a skein of geese coming low for me out of a January dawn, or the bustle of a rising grouse as he jumps from the heather).

The float begins to glide along, submerging as it goes, not with the silly vacuous bobbing of a small perch bite, but with a dignity which is all in accord with the mail-clad water-creature at the other end of the line.

In a moment then you will see that the coarse-fisherman (that motionless clod whom the observant spectator can almost imagine to be chewing the cud) becomes a different being, just as the heron, hunched and sleepy-looking, is transformed into a tense feathered assegai ready to strike.

The coiled line travels from the reel, it brings up at last, the hook goes home, and then begins the test of skill.

It is the contrast between the idle sleepy inertness of waiting and these dramatic seconds which epitomises for me the joy of fishing. Once the hook is drawn home and you feel that sullen frantic creature, which you cannot see, striving to escape, then the heart beats a little slower, though excitement is still there, you are still 'keyed up'.

If you are skilful and you play your fish as it should be played, then at last there comes the triumphant moment when he turns upon his side, when he allows himself to be drawn over the net ring and lifted, dripping and exhausted, puffing and amazed, on to the bank.

If he is too small you will return him; if he is large you will either eat him, preserve him for posterity behind glass, or, best of all, take him home and place him in your ornamental garden pond where he will become tame and you can study his beauty and his ways whenever you will.

The majority of anglers despise stuffed fish. It is only the angler who has much of the boy still in him who likes to preserve his big specimens. I must confess at once that I like to do so on occasion, if the work is well and truly done.

It is really far more satisfying aesthetically than eating him. You may gaze upon his bronze or silver bulk during the dour days of winter when thoughts of fishing are far away; you can revive with added clarity the joys of summer water-meads and midge-haunted pools and go over again the waiting and the battle of that far distant day.

But the best way of all is to leave him his right to live, albeit a prisoner, in your garden pond. I rejoice to see my more notable captives disporting themselves under the waterfall which I have constructed for their benefit (and mine).

In the chapters which follow I hope to say something of how big fish may be caught and of the places where I have angled for them, what manner of birds, beasts and wild things I have met with in my solitary vigils; and something too perhaps, of the thoughts which pass through my mind on such tranquil occasions.

CHAPTER II

THORNEY POND

Thoreau, in his *Walden*, describes the enchantment he experienced when fishing at night on Walden Pond. Very few fishermen in Britain fish at night unless they be poachers or carp fishermen. I think this is a pity. I have done a lot of night fishing; indeed some of my most memorable experiences have been during those luminous lonely hours when other men have been snoring in their beds, when even the birds are wrapt in slumber, the bright finches of the sun, the blackbirds and thrushes and the fairy-like warblers. When the sun goes down, however, the birds of darkness stir and go about their business, and many of the water-birds, moorhens and sedge warblers, are also very much awake.

There is a pond not far from my house and which belongs to me where I have done most of my night fishing. It goes by the name of Thorney Pond and is of great antiquity, of monastic origin as are many of the ancient ponds in England.

It is about an acre in extent and is set in the middle of a wilderness of blackthorn jungle and stunted oak and birch. There is a badger's sett under the thickets at the south end, and there are foxes also on the opposite side of the pond. In shape it resembles a pear with the narrow end at the north. There the bottom of the pond shelves gradually and is almost entirely covered with water-lilies which must be almost as old as the pond itself. After heavy floods and wild winters their roots sometimes become detached and, rising to the surface, lie entangled among the lily pads. These roots are immense, of great girth and incredible toughness, bleached a greyish white, resembling the bodies of defunct boa constrictors. Once a fish wins sanctuary there he is safe.

When the lily leaves decay in early winter these floating roots are released. They then drift to the bank and, though appearing to be dead, many shoot forth new green growth in the spring – they seem to possess the vitality of onions.

I have seen Thorney Pond under every change of light, shadow, and season: in winter when the thickets are bare of leaves and I can see through their intricate naked fretwork the distant pastures; in high summer when they are impenetrable green jungles; in spring when the osiers are covered with downy pearls and the black twigs of the blackthorn are covered white as snow with blossom; in autumn when these same bushes are aflame and glowing richly with every conceivable shade of yellow, gold, and pink.

I have seen the pond in 'the bleak midwinter' when it resembles a white billiard-table and the neat prints of hungry moorhens can be traced upon its snow-powdered floor; I have seen it alive and rippling under the breath of blustering winds; but best of all I have seen it in the luminous half-darkness of a midsummer night with drowned stars spangled upon its dark surface.

In the centre it is of great depth. I once put out in my boat with a length of clothes line and an old horseshoe tied to the end and, lowering this over the side, in the very centre of the pond, I paid out thirty feet of cord and failed to touch bottom.

Determined to find its exact depth I then procured more line and touched bottom at thirty-seven feet.

For the most part the sides slope gradually to the centre, save at the western end where the willows grow. Here it drops away more quickly and ten feet from the bank the water is seven feet in depth.

No stream runs into it, but after winter floods a field ditch at the southern end overflows into the pond. It has its

I have seen the pond in 'the bleak midwinter' when it resembles a white billiard-table

seasonal rise and fall, and after a dry summer the level drops three feet or so. I have never known it drop more than four feet. The water is of crystal clearness, but in places I am troubled by dense blankets of an under-surface pond weed which spreads with great rapidity over all the shallower parts. The centre, though, always remains wide open and intensely dark like a black eye.

Every summer I have to spend a day or so clearing this weed, which I do with a grapnel and a rake, piling it into the flat-bottomed boat which soon sinks to the gunwales with the weight. Pond weed is very heavy stuff to move because of its water content. But it comes away easily enough.

If I did not check its growth it would, in a couple of seasons, make fishing from the bank quite impracticable.

The fish in Thorney Pond are carp, perch, tench, roach, and rudd. I also once put in fifty rainbow trout. These latter fish, when I put them in, averaged three quarters of a pound. Three years later I caught two trout, one on a worm when I was fishing for tench, the other on a fly. The first fish weighed two pounds and a quarter, the second was a little under that weight. I have caught none since nor have I seen a single trout. Whether they have been killed by otters, eels, or herons, or have simply died out, I cannot say, but the fact remains that they have completely disappeared. Rainbow trout are migratory fish and are never happy in a land-locked pond; they cannot breed without spawning beds, and they need a good supply of runnning water if they are to thrive.

There have been carp and tench in Thorney Pond for many years – it is not known who introduced them. I put in one hundred mirror and common carp myself, a dozen years back, and these have grown fast; but when I first purchased the pond it already contained very large fish. Carp delight in a deep and weedy water, but they also like extensive areas of shallow where they may bask and spawn. Old clay-pits are eminently suitable for this species as long as there is weed.

I did no stocking with tench as they have always been abundant, and I wish the rudd and perch elsewhere though they are pretty little fish. In Thorney Pond they grow to no size; the best I have caught is a pound and a half, the average four or five ounces. Like the tench they have been in the pond for many years.

When I first bought the property it was a veritable wilderness; the water was choked with weed and the timber had had no attention. I set to work with saw and bagging-hook and cut winding paths among the blackthorn thickets, and these paths in summer I keep mown with a scythe.

At the southern end I erected a small wooden hut among the trees. In this I have a bed. I frequently sleep there during the summer when I am doing any night fishing.

I have grown very fond of Thorney Pond. Not only do I delight in the water itself: the winding paths among the thickets have an especial charm during the months of early summer. There is something very primitive in this attraction. I have noticed how my children love to follow their deviations (I remember as a boy I took the same keen delight in following sheep and cattle tracks on the Berkshire downlands).

The dense blackthorn thickets, the peace and the quiet, attract a great many birds. The ones I love most are the bullfinches and turtledoves. These latter gentle doves, whose form and soft colouring are so refined and exquisite, arrive early in May. I eagerly listen for their peaceful purrings, one of the chief summer sounds about Thorney Pond. Very early in the June mornings, when I am lying on my bed in the hut with the door wide open and the window also, I hear their lullabies soon after dawn begins to pale in the eastern sky. The first birds to sing are the thrushes. Soon after two o'clock of a mid-June morning I hear their initial muted flutings, and very soon the blackbirds begin to warble. (It may seem a heresy to some when I say that I prefer the mature rich warbling of a June blackbird to a choir of nightingales. There was one that used to come to a large hawthorn behind my hut and the round melodious notes seemed to fill my humble room.) Others answer from various parts of the little wilderness about me, for the blackbird's song in spring and early summer is as much a challenge as that of a crowing cock. I have watched this bird from my window, perching among the masses of ivory hawthorn blossom, his sleek black coat making a rare contrast to the flowery bower in which he sits, his bright orange bill being the only note of vivid colour. Of the nine species of 'black' inland birds – raven, rook, jackdaw, carrion, hoodie, ring ousel, moorhen, coot, dipper – the quality of the black in a cock blackbird's plumage is the most beautiful. It is a deep, deep, soft black, like velvet, with no scintillating gloss such as is found in the crow tribe. He sings with every fibre of his being, and after his lovely descant he will turn his head and listen, his bright dark eye alert and questioning.

Blackcaps are common; their tinkling, echoing song has something of water-music in it. Unlike other birds they sing all day, even in the heat of green noon. Very soon I hear the soft pipes of the bullfinches. These lovely little finches with the Roman noses are true birds of the blackthorn thickets and one does not often see them; only the weaving white spot above the tail is glimpsed for a moment as they dive from one green jungle to another – it is like the diminutive 'flag' of an elfin deer.

I am sure that a white spot on the tail of an animal or a bird acts as a guiding mark for their young. The moorhens possess it, and after that distinctive beacon their dusky blackamoor babies scramble as the mother bird threads the sombre jungles of the reeds.

The jay possesses the same vivid 'flag' – again a bird of dense thickets.

Sometimes, as I lie awake on summer nights, I hear the merry 'cruiks' of the moorhens, who seem just as busy at night as during the day. Occasionally too there comes the sudden startling splash of a big carp. These fish delight in leaping suddenly upwards, as salmon do, especially in the early part of the summer when the breeding time has come. Later, when summer has grown weary and the oaks put forth their vitreous green new leaves at the tips of their branches, the fish become quiescent.

Another sound of spring is the concert of the frogs. They come to Thorney Pond in their thousands. The pilgrimage begins in early March or, in a mild season, in February, and as the spring advances the number of lowly pilgrims swells. In early April the margins of the pond are a churning writhing mass as the male frogs grip their consorts in a vice-like hold.

Another resident is the woodpigeon. There are few more beautiful sounds than a number of ringdoves cooing in concert; as with the blackbirds, it is a form of challenge. It is amazing also to notice how the voices of the ringdoves vary, how some coo at a different pitch from others.

But to return to my blackbird which sang to me by the hut. He invariably ended his warbling song with a sweet musical refrain which was particularly pleasing. Once I took with me a pencil and paper so that I might write it down. Here it is:

I was therefore able to locate him wherever he happened to be singing, in any part of the little wood. For three seasons he came and I looked forward eagerly to his arrival. This was especially so after the terrible winter of 1947 when countless thousands of birds of every kind perished in the arctic cold and unyielding frost and snow. Alas! – when April came I heard him not. Other blackbirds came, those fortunate birds which had somehow survived that sad time, but I listened in vain for the familiar haunting staves.

That same dread winter wiped out all the green woodpeckers and most of the tree creepers, and never once, during the spring of 1947, did I hear that glad, wild, woodland clarion sounding from the oaks. The crevices of bark had been glazed with frost, and their staple food supply locked securely away.

Thorney Pond was devoid of any bird life during that winter. I looked in vain for the tracks of moorhens on the snow-powdered ice; not a pigeon came to the oaks as they normally do; and the only spoor I found was that of rabbit and fox.

There were signs of badger activity. The sett, a very ancient (and I should say impregnable) stronghold in the steep south bank is under the roots of a stunted oak tree. The entrance is large enough for my four-year-old daughter to crawl into.

Just before the onset of the cold, I went one December twilight to see if I could bag a duck for my supper as these shy, much-persecuted birds occasionally visit Thorney Pond in the shooting season.

The pond itself was frozen over, though the ice was not then very thick. I noticed a quantity of dried grass and leaves lying at the foot of the bannk and some of it upon the ice – there was enough to fill two heaped barrows.

Across the ice, from one bank to the other, were the marks of the badger's claws; they had beaten quite a trail. Opposite, at the foot of the bank, was a mass of dead grass and drifts of oak and willow leaves. The cleanly beasts had evidently been busy changing their bedding. This shows that badgers do not enter into a deep winter sleep as many suppose, and it also indicates that these wise and secretive animals had sensed the approach of the unusually bitter spell which did not break until late in March.

These badgers are very bold. I cannot say for sure how many inhabit the sett under the oak, but there is one very large boar badger and a small one which visit my hut regularly during the summer nights.

When I have cooked my supper (usually fish of my own catching) I put the refuse in an old pail which I keep for the purpose behind the hut. At about two in the morning I hear the sound of snufflings and muffled gruntings, and the clang of the metal bucket. They usually upset it and devour anything they can find which happens to be in it; old crusts, coffee grounds, fish bones, apple peelings, and so on – all are eaten.

Though they come so brazenly, and though, with their keen sense of smell, they must be aware of me lying in the hut a few feet from them, they do not attempt to scavenge quietly; but should I make any movement on my bed, if they but hear the creak of a floor board or a stealthy footfall, they are off, vanishing like smoke into the dark thickets.

One night, however, hearing them busy at their supper, I managed to reach the door, and shining my powerful electric torch round the angle of the hut I dazzled them in its glare. The big boar badger was on his hind legs with his muzzle in the bucket. The smaller one, probably a female, was close beside him. When the sudden glare of light leapt upon them from the darkness she must have been in the act of devouring a potato peeling, for she faced me with her striped head raised and one large strip of peel hanging across her nose.

For a moment they were frozen, like two statues, the big boar badger with his muzzle still in the bucket but making no movement of head or body. Then with a crash the pail was overturned and my two dear wild wood-bears lumbered away into the darkness. They did not come the next night, but the night after that I heard them at the bucket again. This time I forbore to disturb them.

Up to the winter of 1947 owls were common and they used at times to disturb my slumbers by their incessant hootings. But they suffered as badly as the green woodpeckers and are only just beginning to return.

It is my firm belief that tawny owls are great fishermen. A pair of tawnies used to nest in the oak above the badger's sett. Climbing up one day I found in the cavity above, the traces of fish bones and a half-eaten carp, a fish of about two pounds.

It is a mystery to me, however, how the owls manage to catch the fish. They must wait for them at night, like kingfishers, upon the overhanging boughs of the oak, and pounce down upon them as the carp come routing along the black margin of the pond. Owls are certainly fond of bathing, and I remember one night, some years ago, hearing something splashing in the water where the willows grow. The moon was shining brightly (it was near midsummer). I saw a large object flapping and fluttering, sending the spray in all directions. For a time I thought it was some animal, but no animal I could identify, until at last it flew up on to a dead branch of the willow and I saw that it was a tawny owl. He shook out his feathers like a fowl after a dust bath, and them flew silently off into the trees.

When summer is done and the thickets show their bare bones, when the acorns drop from the oaks and the mellow October mists lie thick over the water meadows, I look and listen for the first arrival of the winter migrants. By that time the carp have gone down into the deep water, rafts of multi-coloured leaves drift upon the surface of the pond, and one might think there were no fish in the place. In early November the redwings arrive and begin to feast upon the berries, and after them come the handsome 'felts' or fieldfares. Thorney Pond is a favourite roosting place for the redwings, and often when I am there in the late autumn dusk I disturb them from the bushes bordering the paths, and they blunder out with a great to-do, beating their wings upon the thorns. Odd pheasants come at this ripe time in search of acorns, and I get an occasional woodcock, though they are few and far between and almost always come just before a heavy fall of snow.

I have a good stock of rabbits. These Thorney Pond rabbits are very dark in the fur; some are almost black;

many are 'stub' rabbits which do not seem to live in holes. The countrymen say that stub rabbits are more toothsome than those that live in the warrens; those I sometimes shoot at Thorney Pond are certainly of excellent flavour. It is strange that the rabbit should take to lying out like a hare. Huntsmen say that there are definitely 'stub' foxes which rarely kennel in an earth, but prefer a pollard willow or hollow stump in which to sleep. It may be my imagination, but I fancy my 'stub' rabbits are much shorter in the ear and longer in the fur than their warren cousins.

In October, when I have finished with my angling for the season and my rods are put away, I sometimes go and sleep in the hut. I arrive at Thorney Pond in the afternoon with my gun and spaniel, and hunt the thickets through. I can usually count on a shot at a pheasant in that month, and I never fail to get a rabbit.

My habit is to take up station with my gun among the willows. From there I can cover the whole northern bank. I send the spaniel off into the thickets, and from long practice he knows just what to do. He works his way towards me and very soon I see the rabbits, disturbed from their ash stubs and thorny beds, loppiting along the bare red bank. If I am lucky I hear the sudden uprush of a pheasant and his loud hysterical 'cocking' as he rockets up over the oaks. Most of these stray birds come my way, bound for the stubbles outside my wood, and I get some very pretty shots as they come steadily over, tail streaming behind, and the mellow autumn sunlight gleaming on their glittering breasts of mail.

Sometimes, when hit, they plummet straight into the pond, and then my spaniel has to swim, the sort of retrieve he loves more than any other. Sometimes they crash into the bushes behind me. Whatever I shoot, rabbit or pheasant, I then go back to the hut and build a fire. I pluck or skin my game and cook it on the spot, just as I cook and eat any sizeable fish I am fortunate enough to catch.

At such times, when I am sitting beside the embers of my fire after a dinner of my own hunting, with my pipe drawing sweetly and my dog beside me, I feel that this is the most natural life for a man. We are, I believe, solitary hunters by nature. Primitive man always hunted by himself in the woods – the lone hunter has a greater chance of securing game.

I look upon the calm surface of the pond where the gold leaves are floating, at the snug log cabin behind me, at the half-bare oaks and willows, and know with a curious inner satisfaction that evey leaf, every stick, every acorn, in this two-acres-and-a-half of ground is all mine own. I own it as completely as the fox his earth or the badger his sett.

I have around me wild creatures, both in the pond and out of it, which share with me this, 'mine own sole ground', and I think I am more happy and content than the most wealthy landed squire or baron in the land.

Here indeed are the mellow fruits that this life has to offer, and as I sit by my fire and watch the light die over the oaks I think sorrowfully of other men less fortunate who live in the great towns, whose tastes are similar to mine, and how they never will, in all this life, taste of the delights which I am enjoying with such gusto.

This mellow time of October is, more than any other, the month of the hunter. I always regret that the fishing then is done, that I must wait for so long before I gain try my skill with the finny Trolls which inhabit the pond.

I know that when October is out my hut will be locked up and the place will be deserted save for an occasional visit with the gun and possibly a friend. I do not know Thorney Pond so intimately then, when I am back in the bosom of my family with my wife and children.

But how good, how *right* it is that a man should, once in a while, be able to get away from the humdrum business of life, to lead this Utopian existence, even if only for an odd night and day once a month. How good it is for the mind and soul!

There are no smoother reaches in life's stream than these when one is close to Nature, living in a natural way. The fires and follies of love, so-called wordly pleasures, do not touch this inner peace. There are truly times when a man wishes to be away from women, away from even his fellow men. There must be no distracting thought or passion to disturb that serenity. He can be solitary with his own thoughts; the whole purpose of life becomes more plain to him, and even the fact of death itself is not disturbing, since it is the way of all nature, and what is natural is completely in accord with the universe and the architecture thereof.

How shallow at such times seem to be the bickerings of man and man, country and country, in what a mean light we see ourselves!

There is something in the sound of the night wind in the trees and the cluck of a moorhen on the pond which tells me there is nothing in the world to worry about; that theCreator has given us for a short fraction of time the opportunity to achieve this ease and peace of mind, and has said, 'Here, look upon this lovely place where Nature manifests itself, and mark well the beauty of my handiwork'.

The dog heaves a sigh of contentment (he has had his supper), the rose-red embers of my fire rustle and fall asunder, and I am content to seek my bed in the little hut and know that all is well with man and with the world.

It often amuses me to watch my dog enjoying the company and cheer of our campfire. A cat will curl up and go to sleep; it is not mesmerised as the dog is by the glowing core of a fire's heart.

My spaniel sits upright, his eyes fixed on the embers, burrs from his afternoon's hunting still matted in his feathers. He stares and stares at the crumbling caverns of the fire-landscape, and perhaps pursues phantom fire-rabbits, maned and ragged as heraldic lions, among the palaces and passages of that brilliant crumbling ruin.

At last even he wearies, the head drops, the eyes half close, sleep is busy with his brain. He sways a little, one foot half-gives under the weight of his body, and he rouses himself to stare again.

Twice, thrice, this happens, until, in desperation, and with another deep breath, he surrenders to the summons, turns around once or twice with his nose in his tail, and settles himself with a final sigh of contentment and peace.

On many occasions, after an afternoon and evening's hunting, we have thus dropped off beside our open hearth, and I have awakened gradually to find the dark night about us, the embers dead and my body chilled. I have gazed for a moment or two in uncomprehending amazement at the trembling points of stars above, and listened to the night breeze busy in unseen tree tops close at hand.

CHAPTER III

NIGHT FISHING AT THORNEY POND

Though, as might be guessed, I find a great measure of enjoyment in these autumn excursions to Thorney Pond, they are hardly to be compared with my nocturnal vigils during the nights of the latter half of June and in July.

The great carp do not begin to feed until the end of the former month: they are, I think, too busy with the excitement and bustle of the mating season. In late spring this embowered water echoes with their leapings. I have seen one, presumably a male, pursuing another all over the pond; I have marked the arrowing wakes, the miniature wash, as the big fish charge hither and thither in all directions. But, like the frogs, when the mating season has passed and their spirits are eased, they abandon themselves to other pleasures, the chief of which is basking in the warm upper layer of water. On still hot days when the air is loud with the deep hum of millions of insects, they loll in mid-water, singly and in pairs, sometimes in a shoal, motionless and seemingly asleep, as snug and lazy as cats before a kitchen grate, completely bewitched by their summer life.

The best view one can have of these fish at such a time is from the mound above the badger sett. They can then be seen like so many blue-grey balloons, lying motionless just under the surface; and occasionally, if the sun is very hot, one will thrust forth its back, which is as shining and smooth as that of a porpoise. Though they appear a leaden hue in the water, when on the bank (which occasionally happens) there is no trace of this cloudy, somewhat muddy hue. They are then seen to be beautiful bronze fish, short and thick, with small heads and considerable breadth of body. The mirror carp, which grow to a larger size, and have few scales upon their flanks, are more drab – some indeed have the smoky appearance one notices in the water. The very large specimens are ugly, even repulsive to the inexperienced and unsympathetic eye.

The best times for catching carp are either early morning or late at night, and when the weather is very warm the small hours are the most productive.

I usually arrive at Thorney Pond a little after nine o'clock on a late June evening, choosing a night after a day of heat. My first action is to throw in some ground-bait either broken lob worms or bread-paste balls. I then go back to the hut and cook my supper, attended as usual by my dog.

This meal is almost always eggs and bacon, or sausage and fried potato, followed by an apple and a glass of good ale drawn from my own barrel at home and carried to my camp in an earthenware-stoppered jar.

Supper over and the plates and other things safely stowed away, I return to my pitch to begin operations. I might say at once that ordinary tackle is useless for dealing with such doughty adversaries as these Thorney Carp. Other anglers who occasionally try their skill (with my permission) are invariably broken by these big fish, which average six and seven pounds apiece. Some are a good deal larger. The mirror carp seem much heavier, and I have seen one or two which must be in the region of twenty pounds.

The rod which I use for the big carp is a Hardy 'Palakona'. The reel was specially made by a friend, R.W., a skilful carp-fisher, who occasionally comes to stay with me; a man whose tastes are very similar to mine and who takes as keen a delight as I do in the joys of my solitary pond. I will describe this reel later.

On these notable occasions he wears a wondrous hat of

felt, not unlike a massive thimble, its brim ragged and worn as though the water-rats had been at it. The history of this hat deserves passing mention:

When R.W. was an undergraduate at Caius he happened one day to be out on the river when a University crew were practising. Along the towpath rode the coach, the President of the University Boat Club, and a puckish gust of wind blew the hat from his head. It landed in the river close to R.W., who retrieved it. He sent a note to the owner telling him that he had the hat safely in his rooms and that if he would care to come and collect, R.W. would be glad. For some reason or other the owner never bothered to come, and so R.W. now wears it as a sort of lucky charm and swears he has caught bigger and better fish when he has been wearing it. This certainly holds true of his effort at Thorney Pond, as last year he landed a seventeen-pound mirror carp and thereby holds the record for the pond.

It is not often, however, when I fish through the dark hours, that I have a companion other than my dog; indeed I find that half the magic is lost if there is anyone with me. Even though your expert carp-fisher is one of the most inoffensive and silent of men, a lover of solitude and quietness, such a one is not always welcome.

Behold us then, my dog and I, cautiously approaching the baited pitch which is on the left of the willows at the south end. There is a little promontory there of fine green grass, a sort of miniature table on which I sit. I am screened from the pond by a slender lattice of willow wands, boughs I have plucked myself from the nearby tree and stuck into the leaf-mould margin of the water where they have taken root.

It is most essential to have a screen when one is trying for the big fish. I have seen ignorant anglers actually *holding* their rods and standing up on the bank without any cover whatever. They, needless to say, never have a bite.

I stick my rod rest in the grass plateau and place the butt of the 'Palakona' therein. This rest is a length of stout annealed wire some two feet long and at the top is a clip in the shape of a Grecian harp. The rod rests on the narrow waist and the line below is quite free from any danger of being nipped between rest and rod.

Upon my reel (of which I shall have more to say in a later chapter) I have one hundred yards of dressed silk line of 10lb. breaking-strain, the strongest I can obtain without its being too obvious in the water. To this is attached either my worm cast and float (the latter cocked by a single round shot); or, if I am fishing by the floating bread method, as I usually do at night, I tie the hook direct to the line by a blood loop. If I am fishing floating crust, I cut a piece off the loaf about three inches across and draw the hook through it so that the barbed side is half hidden by the crumb. A diagram will make this plain:

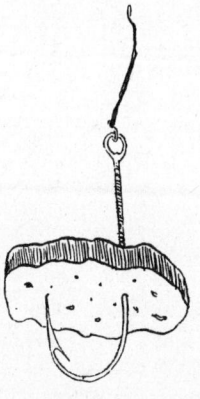

Dipping this crust into the water to give it weight without loosening and dissolving it, I cast it out a little way, not more than seven feet or so from the bank.

At night the big carp come close inshore and they will methodically patrol the edges of my little mere as if they were night watchmen.

At times if I decide to bait with worm I cast this farther out so that my float is more visible. Float fishing is more satisfying than fishing a floatless line and crust, but I get bigger fish by the latter method.

It is wise to use a big quill, and as dusk deepens I find it necessary to fasten a feather in the rubber cap band. It is amazing how visible this is long after all other objects have become obscure. But on a dark night and against tree reflections even the feather is at last unseen and one can only fish by ear and touch. Your line is drawn off the reel, about two yards of it is coiled carefully on the grass, and if a big carp takes your bait your first warning is the sudden scream of the reel.

Some anglers tie a scrap of white material to the line;

others use luminous floats. I have never found the latter particularly good.

Having cast out my worm bait I will often fish this until darkness has practically come, when I change to the floating bread.

At midsummer the nights are brief, the last sunset glow does not die until near midnight BST, and within an hour the east is beginning to pale.

My float cast forth, I sit down behind my willow screen and smoke my pipe. In the windless air the fragrant blue vapour solemnly ascends, driving the dancing midge clouds to one side. The time is now a little past 10 p.m. and there is barely a sign as yet of the onset of night. These summer twilights are interminable and the current of all life seems to flow more slowly. All through the noonday heats there has been a hum up in the tree tops (later in the summer, in the afternoon of the year, this hum is increased a millionfold, but in late June there are not so many insects and the flies do not worry one so much). Now that hum has died and there are few sounds to break the quiet.

Over the oak tops a heron comes gliding, his great wings cupped and sensitive to his every movement. For the last hour, while I have been busy preparing supper, he has been circling round, watching me from afar, uttering from time to time indignant harsh cries at seeing his sanctuary invaded. Now he believes me gone; he does not, cannot, see me behind my veil of willows, nor can he spy the lemon-and-white spaniel sitting by my side. Over the tree tops he comes, rocking a little as a homing bomber will do just before its wheels touch the runway. Up go the great wings high above his head, the body tilts vertically, and the long green claws grasp the half-sunken log, where he always stands, with gentle sureness. Then those precious wings are neatly folded, much as a man folds an umbrella, and for a little while he stands very straight and slim, searching his surroundings with his great eye. Finding that all is quiet, he stalks with nodding head down the sloping log and after a while his head sinks down. He looks twice the bird he was.

The moorhens come swimming out from the reeds, their heads jerking. They seem to make an effort of swimming, so different from the wild mallard who glide about the water as though propelled by screws, sometimes reversing with equal grace. They peck this side and that among the lily pads, and maybe perch upon some bleached and fixed lily root in pheasant-like attitudes, preening themselves, and conversing from time to time in watery, happy clucks and quirks.

From my secret spy-hole among the willow wands I can observe how contented and happy are these various tenants of mine, how much more at ease they are now that they believe they have the pool to themselves. It saddens me at times that the human form should spell such dread among the wild things. And then I remember the stricken pheasant plummeting down in the glory of his pride; the head-over-heels rabbit; the desperate tuggings of a fighting fish – I have only myself to blame....

So strange and twisted is this hunting instinct! If the pheasant stalked up to me boldly and unafraid, if the rabbit came fearlessly to nibble the grass beside me, how could I ever shoot again! The lion would lie down with the lamb.

I can well sympathise with the edible wild creatures, and how I should flee in terror at that upright two-legged form in its drab garments, the pale spot of the face and the two pale spots of the hands – how the sight of it would fill me with unnameable dread! And yet I know that there are fellow creatures whom they dread far more. The rabbit is stricken helpless with fear at the sight of a stoat, the wild pigeons are frantic should a hawk appear. I have had them dive down into the trees beside me when a hawk has flown among them. I have seen partridges crouching close at hand, with no fear of me, but terror of the swift grey bolt of a sparrow hawk which has swooped upon them from over a stack. There have been many instances of small birds fleeing to a man for safety when one of these winged freebooters of the sky dashes upon them.

A memorable sight for me was a skein of greylag geese coming in to a marsh, cackling and happy at the prospect of a feed, when a peregrine dropped out of the sky in one magnificent stoop. The big ungainly birds were like heavy bombers attacked by a waspish fighter plane. They scattered formation. Some dropped like plummets to the marsh and safety; the more foolish lost their heads and flew wildly, raggedly in all directions. No sight of a man with a gun could have spread such panic in those ranks.

The fear of birds for the flesh-eating hawks is very ancient. For a long while man was a comparatively harmless creature, a miserable earth-bound animal who was powerless to kill and pursue.

Wildfowl are far more scared of the appearance of an aeroplane than of a man walking on the ground....

Step by step the night advances over Thorney Pond. The dog beside me is alert, his ears cocked and brow wrinkled. He is far more tense at fall of night than he is during the hours of day, his hunting instinct strongest then. Not a movement escapes his notice, his nose is busy all the time. Occasionally he will shoot a sidelong glance at me as much as to say, 'Master, master, get ready – why are you dreaming there? I smell a rabbit by the pond and moorhens in the reeds; where is your gun?'

Out in the water sits the upright pied quill, a motionless question-mark. Rudd dimple the calm surface, and bubbles breaking in clusters to my right tell of feeding tench. These fish move about in slow-moving shoals – you can mark their passage by the clustering bubbles.

Some years I catch a number of good tench in Thorney Pond and then I have several seasons when I scarcely catch a single specimen. I cannot explain this; it is a mystery which has intrigued generations of anglers. My best catches have been in times of drought when the level of the pond has dropped to its limit. I have never done any good whatever after floods. It is more of a dawn- than a night-feeder, and the best type of morning is during hot weather when a mist lies on the surface, just as the sun begins to climb over the trees.

Of all the coarse fish I admire the tench the most. His lines are exquisite, giving me the same pleasure that I experience when I look at an Oriental carving of a bull in jade, ivory, or bronze. The fins are placed so *rightly* and are of so precise and satisfying a shape; there are no sharp angles. He has not the angular old-maidish tail of a roach or a bream; his tail is rounded at the extremities like the propellors of a ship.

Best of all I admire his neat soft scales and the wonderful deep bronze hue of them. He has the look and feel of the fish aristocrats, the salmon and trout – a perch cannot be compared with him. Pike I cannot abide. It is a truly coarse fish with its cruel shovel mouth and grimly sardonic expression, and the array of needle-like teeth seem to me simply vulgar. Nor do I like his rakish lines and the hard bony nose-plate which rings hollow to the knock of a knuckle. I thank my lucky stars I have none in Thorney Pond, and I live in dread lest they should appear, as they sometimes will, introduced either by the feet of water birds or the mischievous malignance of poaching fishermen.

I have spoken of the underwater weed which is so abundant in Thorney Pond. These cloudy subaqueous cushions can be traced very clearly when one stands high on the bank. Then it is apparent that there are dark unfathomable lanes winding about among this strange vegetation, subways and tunnels which I believe are used regularly by the carp. I remember once standing by the oak tree looking at the sunlit water and I saw a large carp emerge slowly from his deep water tunnel. He came slowly out like an airship from its hangar. I believe they use these tunnels much as rabbits follow their runways in the thick underwood.

Frequently, when I have succeeded in hooking one of these shy and powerful fish, it will straightway make a dash for its burrow and in a few moments the dense weed blanket will bring it to a standstill, which is sometimes a help to the angler rather than a hindrance. Some of the weed, where it is especially thick, lies on the surface, and a crust of bread thrown there will often disappear, drawn below by an unseen mouth.

I believe that carp, and indeed most fish, have a sense of smell. Last year at Thorney Pond I noticed, one sultry August afternoon, that a big carp was moving in the weeds out in the centre. I took a large crust of bread and flung it out. It was a bad shot and landed quite ten feet from where I had seen the movement. For a little while nothing happened. Then I noticed that the weeds again stirred in the same place where I had noticed it before. Gradually those rippling movements drew nearer to the floating bait, the fish seemed to be blindly fumbling through the vegetation, much as a spaniel will follow a scent through almost impenetrable underbrush. Then there was a gulp, a slightly more obvious stir among the clinging weed cushions, and the bait was pulled below.

By now the light has drained from the western sky and already the heron is barely visible, still standing on his log. I have had no bite on the lob worm, so I gently draw it in and change to a floating crust. This is cast forth and hopes run high, for now the magic moment must surely be near.

One or two other crusts are thrown out close to the bank on either hand to act as 'surface bait', and after a while a splashing scrum of little rudd attack the bread, buffeting and sucking. They make as much noise about it as schoolboys sucking sweets. A few roach join them.

The stars are lit now, the oak crowns dark and motionless; perhaps from the thickets comes the elfin whirr of a nightjar.

A ripple passes along the bank on the right, and my heart begins to thump painfully for I know what that ripple means. The big carp are now setting out upon their nightly hunt – this is the first of the patrol.

I often wonder whether other fishermen become as excited as I do on such occasions; the suspense is often almost more than I can bear.

It is difficult to see the water now. It is as though my eyes were cloaked by some puckish enchantment, that Robin Goodfellow has squeezed into them some of the magic juice with which Lysander was bemused.

The particles of shattered weed on my right begin to revolve and wander aimlessly: there is certainly a large bulk displacing water there! The rudd scatter in a fright, leaving the white scrap of bread, sodden now with crust half-gone, motionless upon the surface.

Then a whirlpool appears and the crust begins to spin; there is a loud gulping 'cloop', a terrific commotion in the weed. The 'waterbait' has been seized and I know that if I do but remain perfectly still the hook bait will likewise be taken. But this wily unseen monster takes his time. He will swim away to eat the bread and ruminate a little afterwards.

One significant sign – no little rudd are scrimmaging at my hook bait. It lies white and still, the deadly barb crouching in hiding, an assassin in ambush.

This interval is agonising. I advise all those anglers who suffer from weak hearts to abstain from carp fishing at night, for they are far more likely to quit this twilit world than the carp they seek to slay.

Sometimes the climax comes without any warning. The weeds part, the bait is snuffed out, and the next instant your rod point is bowed to the very surface of the pond.

There is nothing so exciting in all the various forms of

fishing, either in salt water or fresh, than the first impetuous rush of a hooked carp.

His power is enormous, his initial run is sometimes as long as a hundred yards, if he is a big one and you are fishing fairly 'light'.

In the summer of 1947 I was night fishing at Thorney in August and the carp were on the move. The rudd that night were particularly trying, buffeting and devouring my bait as soon as it touched the water so that in a few minutes it was completely sodden and useless.

I got over the difficulty by fishing close inshore and drawing up my crust so that it dangled a fraction above the surface of the pool. Even then the rudd made gallant efforts to seize it, playing 'bob apple' with it and thrusting forth their eager little jewelled faces to get at it.

When I noticed the whorls approaching, I lowered the bait on the surface of the pond by one click of the reel. The next instant an enormous face appeared, a face which reminded me of one of Blake's monsters in his illustrations to the *Book of Job*.

It came blindly pushing forward, a streamer of weed shielding its piggy greedy eyes, and wavering ever nearer it mouthed the suspended bait, then bolted with it in a shower of spray.

I failed to land this fish. What weight he was I have no idea, but he must have been one of the twenty-pounders. He beat me by going round some obstruction six feet down, possibly a snag and one that was known to him. But break me he did and that most successfully, departing with ten feet of line and my hook entire.

Carp take a variety of baits. In some waters small potatoes, the kind one throws away or gives to the pigs, are very killing, but they must be boiled and peeled and the hook threaded with a baiting needle. Wasp grubs are also good, worms a sure standby, and all manner of pastes, sweetened and unsweetened, are taken at times.

It all depends on what the carp have been educated to. In one carp water where I fish worms are useless – I have never had a bite with them – but large balls of bread-paste never fail to provide sport of some sort.

There was a mirror carp in Thorney Pond which seemed always to be swimming on his own. He had no scales whatever on his flanks which were a rather unusual shade of rich chestnut brown (it is amazing how 'mirrors' vary in coloration). Every evening he made a tour of the southern end, and after a while I came to look for him taking his constitutional. Most fish like plenty of exercise.

This carp had a particularly chubby and benign expression and was by nature intensely curious. When the leaves began to fall I still observed him on mellow afternoons, swimming close to the surface, turning aside now and again to examine floating willow leaves, some of which he took into his mouth and expelled again after a little while.

I thought I would try to catch him with a floating crust, though he did not appear to me to be a big fish (I put him at about two pounds, but it is hard to judge their weight when they are in the water. As a general rule, by close observation, you can double their apparent weight).

Your really big fish has a small head and the shoulders slope steeply like that of a perch; the body is not unduly long compared with the size of the head; his depth you cannot see owing to the refraction of the light. But watch until he turns stern on to you. If it appears wide and balloon-like, then he is a big fish.

One afternoon in early September when I was gathering nuts close to the hut I spied my friend swimming along his usual beat, and I determined to try and catch him. My rod was in the hut and was quickly assembled; the hook was attached to the line and baited with a large crust, and I swung it out fairly near the bank. The light breeze which was blowing drifted it out and before long I spied 'Old Chestnut' approaching. He first came past the crust about six inches down and appeared to take no notice. Then he caught sight of it, turned about and made a circle round it, coming closer as he did so. He approached it from downwind as carp usually do, possibly guided by smell rather than sight, and took it at a gulp.

The line travelled out, I struck, and after a lively tussle landed him, not without some difficulty as the bank was steep just there. He proved to be four pounds, exactly double his estimated weight. I returned him at once.

This floating bread method is very killing in the majority of carp waters. The difficulty of getting the bait well out is the greatest drawback, but if the line is thoroughly greased and the crust is not too sodden, and one has a light backing breeze, one can float it out fifty yards or more, right among a basking school of fish. You pay the line off the reel as the crust goes out.

Carp will frequently take a floating bait on a hot day when the sun is shining. It is a very skilful and exciting form of fishing.

One thing is essential – a capacious landing net. Many specimen fish have been lost through this simple lack, for the ordinary-sized landing net is worse than useless. R.W., of the magic hat, has on more than one occasion lost good fish because his net was too small. Those large salmon landing-nets that are used exclusively on some Scotch rivers are the thing.

I know no coarse fish capable of such a fierce and protracted rush when he feels the hook; it equals the charge of a spring salmon. The average rustic fishermen go in terror of large carp, for should they hook one it invariably means the loss of the major part of their tackle and in some instances the rod as well!

I know a pond in Hertfordshire where large mirror carp are found, and where an inexperienced angler who left his rod unattended on the bank was taught a memorable lesson. He heard a splash while he was down at the other end of the pool, and looking up saw his rod hurtling through the air javelin-wise. It disappeared under the surface; it was never seen again!

To the nocturnal angler there comes a moment when all fishy movement ceases, when even the creatures of darkness seemed awed to immobility and the air of the warmest summer night takes on a sudden deathly chill. It is that hour when Nature is at its lowest ebb, the hour when so many mortals relinquish hold on life and pass over to that Bourne which awaits us all.

The sudden change is uncanny. Before midnight everything seems watchful and alert; even the mysterious shadowy trees seem to regard one suspiciously. But in that passage of time between one in the morning and cockcrow the pulsing fires of life seek some warm retreat, the blessedness of sleep.

On a calm June night the stars are sometimes very brilliant, intensified by the black and rounded coronets of the trees.

It is hard to believe, as I lie in my hut watching those flickering pale points which have no cheerfulness nor warmth in them, that in great cities men are labouring in the glare and rattle of machinery. Such activity seems outrageous, an affront to Nature. Night workers always have my deepest sympathy and admiration.

When the weather is warm I sleep with the hut door open wide, the window also, and it is interesting to lie snug in my camp bed listening to those very small and furtive vibrations which steal upon the ear from time to time. It is fascinating to guess what manner of creature is the cause, or what law of Nature is in operation and is so manifesting itself.

With my dog breathing steadily at the foot of the bed, I am never conscious of my solitary state, nor do I often have any sense of mistrust or fear.

Every rustle of leaf is magnified; even the perambulations of insects are audible. A hunting hedgehog or mouse can be heard very plainly and from a considerable distance. Once as I lay staring out of the door at the faint glimmer of the Pond a dim round object appeared on the threshold and peered inquiringly in. At first I thought it must be a rabbit, or a large rat; but soon I saw that it was a hedgehog on his evening prowl, and it amused me to see him scratch himself on his furry underneath with a dog-like action of his back paw.

Another time I was awakened by a strange clanking sound outside the hut and thought that one of the badgers must be raiding the waste pail. But it was a small, sharp, metallic noise and could not have been caused by so large a creature. Much mystified I got out of bed and, pulling on my trousers, stepped out in my bare feet on to the cold and dew-wet grass. I found that a hedgehog had discovered my worm-tin, which I had carelessly left lying by the side of the hut with the lid removed. Smelling the worms therein he had thrust in his little slender snout to win himself a cheap meal.

Some sound maybe had disturbed him, or he had suddenly panicked. They are intensely nervous creatures, and when suspicious the tiniest sound (they have very keen ears) makes them erect their spines. This he had done, and as his head and shoulders were confined in the narrow cylinder of tin he had found himself held fast as if in the stocks.

Frantically he was endeavouring to free himself, and the sight of that animated tin from which protruded two pinkish legs was one of the most laughable things I have ever seen.

In late July the young tawny owls frequently keep me awake with their wheezing incessant cries for food. Yet I like to hear their bronchial hunger-cries, now close at hand now faint and far as they fly to the distant oaks on the far side of the Pond. All young creatures seem to take a delight in a reiterated sharp cry. Young bullfinches pipe incessantly when they have left the nest. The pipe is half a chirp and has an amazing carrying power. They are at it all day long from four in the morning until sunset. By 10 p.m. in mid-July their hunger is appeased – it is the only time they are silent save when they snatch a brief nap after a feed. Yet how necessary it is that they should perpetually cry in this way, for the parents would have no other means of locating them in the dense green arbours which they so dearly love.

I often see them during the latter end of the summer, perching on the willow, piping their hunger-cry. At each pipe the head is pushed forward and the short stub tail is slightly raised. The bird pipes with its whole body, like a mechanical toy. Young moorhens are also vociferous; so are greenfinches and goldfinches. The latter follow the parents wherever they go, keeping up a continual sharp twittering which after a time is quite maddening to the human ear. But what a pretty sight it is to see a brood of these gay finches, which seem to have sunlight in their plumage; what an exquisite clear yellow are the bands upon their wings; what a perfect contrast are the black-and-white pied spots on the tips of the primaries!

Most infant wild animals are mute, though I have heard young badgers calling plaintively to their parents when out for their evening stroll. Should one happen to be left behind he raises the most piteous imploring cries.

What a wise dispensation of Nature it is that when actually in the nest most birds are silent. The bullfinch and greenfinch do not start crying for food until they can fly, and even when the parents come with food the nestlings raise but a minute, threadlike cheep which can only be heard if you happen to be standing within a foot or so of the thickets. I have many times discovered a nest of fledgling bullfinches in this way.

One notable exception is that of young tits and starlings. The latter begin to 'churr' for food when only a few days old. These birds, however, build in holes, in trees or buildings, where they are comparatively safe from harm unless some bold rat or stoat happens to chance that way and can climb up to them. Stoats are adept at climbing, and

I have seen them running as nimbly as squirrels up the fork of a tall ash tree.

Even small children seem to take a pleasure in reiterated cries.

Sometimes when I have been sitting by my willow during these night watches which are so valuable to me, I have heard, high above, the bumbling hum of an areoplane and have seen its port and starboard lights move across the dim vault overhead, two animated and synthetic stars against the cold pale streamer of the Milky Way.

I have conjured up the picture of that throbbing air-machine, the intricate lighted dials of the cockpit, the perilous enclosed cabin where men and women are maybe reading newspapers or conversing together, comfortably seated in their well-upholstered seats, or maybe being served with cocktails by a white-coated steward. I wonder at its destination: it may be India or Africa, Paris, or Vienna.

These big air liners possess the romance and drama of the old sailing ships yet are far more wonderful. It amuses me to let my imagination range from that long illuminated cabin to this secret well, four thousand feet below, where I sit among the night trees waiting for a carp.

From time to time I hear the smacking 'suck suck' of a big fish busy in the weeds, and the reflection of a star is rocked and split by ripples widening outwards.

When the night is very dark one cannot see even the white cube of bread floating a few feet away, and then the only thing to do is to feel cautiously with the fingers for the line, coiled while there was yet light so carefully on the grass. If a fish takes your bait and rushes of with it and feels the slightest check during those first few feet, he will expel the bait with one gigantic puff.

It is wise to have a shaded electric torch for night fishing. This is essential when the line has to be coiled, for sooner or later one is bound to get some tangle in the line which it is impossible to unravel without artificial aid.

R.W. has designed a most ingenious affair for nocturnal carp fishing which has a shielded bulb and a bell which sounds an alarm as soon as the fish rushes off with the bait. The alarm bell is a particularly useful contrivance because it frequently happens that one drops fast asleep when things are slack.

The landing and playing of a heavy carp on a dark night is a most difficult business. One feels the tugging weight of the fighting fish, but one cannot see him save when he makes some extra frantic plunge and throws the spray about.

You cannot see in what direction he is charging and can only play him entirely by feel. Nor is it easy to get him in the net. I have on occasion landed a sunken bough, some flotsam or jetsam of the Pond, in the belief that I had the grandfather of all carp safely in the folds.

As day steals slowly on, the sounds about the hut swell in volume with every passing moment. The birds begin their morning hymns and the wonderful dawn chorus of the woods in May is something which many people have never heard.

How shocking it is that we, in our journey through life, miss out these magic hours of a summer dawn!

By the time the average idle man is abroad the birds have gone forth to seek their breakfasts, and even the world of Nature has lost that first bloom and freshness with which only the camper is familiar.

This is where the early fisherman scores. He enjoys these transitory sights, sounds, and smells. I often think that we waste many precious moments of life within four walls, and that we would be better to sleep, as sleep our bodies must, during the duller and more prosaic noonday hours, as indeed men do in hot climates. For it is then that birds and animals take their rest, even though it is but a short nap snatched at intervals during the arduous business of feeding and rearing their young.

After the dawn lull, I find the fish in Thorney Pond do not feed until the sun is well above the horizon. In late June and July I never expect a bite before seven o'clock, and then for half an hour the carp are sometimes ravenous – I may get six runs in an hour. But should a fish be hooked and lost then I get no more. By some mysterious means the news is telegraphed to the other inhabitants of the Pond, and my float idles motionless among the lily pads.

CHAPTER IV

THE FISHERMAN AND HIS WEAPONS

The observant and sensitive angler can tell at once when he is in a fishing country; not entirely by the sight of lochs, pools, rivers, or drains, but by his conversation with the inhabitants and even by the look of them. I have noticed when passing through some of the fenlands (which are the Mecca of all float-fishers) the eager moustached faces of your true Disciples of Izaak. They have an old-fashioned appearance, dated I think somewhere about the late Edwardian or even Boer War days. These men cling to the straw hat as a form of headgear and are partial to bicycle clips. Most of them, I suspect, are hairdressers by profession. It is not surprising that hairdressers are so often fishermen. They spend their whole lives standing still, and they must also possess great patience. Yet after all, 'patience' does not come into it. It is not patience the angler possesses but an infinite keenness for his sport in which time plays no part at all. Whether he sits for five minutes or for five hours watching his float is of no account to him – indeed waiting might be termed the crust to the pie, the dough to the jam, or use what metaphor you will. If we caught fish every time we went out, if as soon as we put in a line we had to pull it out again because a fish had taken the bait, then all the pleasure would be gone. There indeed would be monotony for you, that indeed would demand patience. That is why sea-fishing has never attracted me. I once went mackerel fishing. My first few victims gave me a certain amount of pleasure, and then the sport was mere butchery. A fisherman is very different from a fish-merchant. Sometimes I have got into a school of small perch, the most stupid and tiresome little fish that swim (when they are hungry, as they usually are), and I feel my enthusiasm dying within me at each cheeky bob and dive of the float.

I suppose that a few so-called fishermen delight in continually catching fish, but they must be men of very coarse fibre. On the other hand I delight to read of a certain carp-fisher who at one time held the record (a 26lb. carp) and who, after years of carp fishing, had a great day and landed four fish, the big one of 26lb., another of 15½, one of 11½, and a mere make-weight of 9½lb. He had to borrow a handcart to take them home. On that occasion at least the scoffers were silenced and with good reason. Not only had he captured all these great fish single-handed, but he had caught them on roach-tackle. Even the landing of the big carp was a triumph which was well deserved, but to bring safely to the bank all the others was indeed something to merit his name being inscribed on the scroll of fame. That was some years ago now; he has, as far as I know, been carp fishing assiduously ever since; but he has come nowhere near his record nor has he again landed more than two big fish in a day.

It is perhaps the knowledge that such things are not beyond the realms of possibility that spurs the angler on, which fixes him even more immovably upon his basket. If I caught big fish every time I went out I should give up angling and confine myself to shooting – rough shooting, not slaughtering half-tame pheasants.

This enthusiasm, this tenacious determination (I will not say patience) is, I think, particularly English, though I have seen the fishermen of the Seine run us pretty close. Yes, 'patience' is entirely the wrong word, as it implies putting up with a thing without complaining for an indefinite time.

I do not complain at being able to sit in a quiet green place with so much beauty around me, with never a dull moment the whole day through; birds to watch, dragon-flies, insects of all kinds; the change of sky, and sun, and shadow; the delightful riverside smells, the grasses and the flowers. Why should I complain? It gives me the keenest delight to observe this world in which I find myself. The study of the grasses alone raises a wonder which should last out the life of a man. And what a perfect time that is in early June when the meadow grasses are at their best, when most have come to flower. The variety and beauty in a few yards of river bank is well worth study. This prodigality of Nature at the flood tide of summer is one of the most wonderful things I know. Every meadow is transformed. To appreciate that wonder, lie down with your face among the countless grass blades and imagine yourself smaller than you are. Our heads are so high above the earth that much of this beauty is passed unheeded. Among the fresh green jungles rise the meadow buttercups, like trees climbing through underwood to the light. How swiftly their boles grow towards the sun until they are above the 'undergrass' and can open their buds to the bright rays, each a varnished yellow cup which moves its petals like the spread wings of a butterfly and closes them for sleep at night.

The majority of people do not even realise that grasses have flowers, flowers so small that only Titania's court could appreciate their beauty. These flowers open at the coming of day (strangely enough those of the Poa grass open in the early dawn between 4 and 5 a.m.). The family is large – some one hundred and thirty species. And when we try to count the various plants, the sorrels, clovers, vetches, and plantains, the mind can hardly think in terms of numbers: it is as overwhelming as thinking of the stars of heaven, or the sands of the sea.

And there are elfin tigers which roam those green miniature forests, deer in the shape of long-tailed field mice, which skip and run like jerboas; weasels and stoats and velvet moles, and insects beyond all computation.

If we could only be Lilliputians for the space of one hour in an English meadow in June, what an experience that would be!

One always finds too that by the waterside the growth of plant and grasses is more thick and abundant and the variety more numerous that out in the open meadows.

The river fisherman of the South and Midlands is perhaps

more fortunate than his Northern brother in this respect. But one cannot really compare the two different types of angling. The fly-fisherman has little time to look at these things: he must always be on the move, his eyes upon his gossamer cast, on the curving fly. He has to watch for the rise of a trout, he must place his fly on the exact spot where he wishes it to go, he must ensure that it drops correctly on the water, copying as far as possible the action of an insect accidently falling in or momentarily alighting.

The knowledge that he is making good casts is in itself a constant source of pleasure. I take a great joy in fly-fishing, but cannot keep at it all day as some men do – I find I miss too much of what is going on around me.

What a delicate difficult art it is, this correct casting of a fly! What a joy it is to watch an expert! Only sensitive men make good fly-fishers, for it calls for an almost feminine touch.

I have often thought it strange that so few women are fond of fly-fishing, and I have only known one keen 'coarse' fisherwoman in my life. I suppose it is because they lack the hunting instinct or they have never had the leisure to master the difficult art.

Without appearing to be at all ungallant I would say that we are happier without our wives and sweethearts when we are engrossed in fishing. They, poor things, know to their cost how meals so carefully and lovingly prepared grow cold upon the table, for no angler is ever punctual at meals. Such gross thoughts as the filling of the belly are not to be entertained for one moment when we are really concerned with catching fish. The soul becomes so enchanted, the body's demands are forgotten.

In boyhood days this is also the case. Even in those early primrose years when, as a general rule, appetite plays an important part, all such things as meal times and food are out of mind. Time does not exist, one is lost in concentration, the eyes have to work hard – indeed, I find that after a long day beside stream or pool my eyes become very strained, though I do not notice that they ache until I have returned home.

I suppose the best-loved rod in my collection is the Hardy 'Palakona' with which I have caught both salmon and large carp. Twelve foot long, weighing just over fourteen ounces, it is the ideal weapon for dealing with heavy fish, and it has the merit of two tops and can be used for either greased line or fly-fishing.

The reel which I use exclusively for carp fishing was made for me by my friend, R.W., and is a lovely thing. He made it himself in his own factory at Letchworth. He tells me that when he managed to get the block of duralumin and was turning it on the lathe, the shavings caught fire. He was enveloped in a mass of flames. If he had let the metal cool it would have been ruined, so he kept at his lathe while everyone else was rushing round trying to put out the fire. A reel which had such a fiery birth is surely destined for great things.

It is very light, weighing only thirteen and a half ounces. It measures five inches and seven-eighths across the drum, with a width of one-and-a-quarter inches. The drum is detachable in a moment by pressing a trigger in the centre. Facing forward is a brake lever which can be applied with the forefinger of the right hand, as I prefer a left-hand wind. But by a quick adjustment of the ratchet inside the drum the reel can be converted to right-hand wind. There is another trigger facing forward which releases the tension, allowing the drum to revolve quite freely. This wide reel has a terrific purchase on a big fish; the line can be drawn in with great rapidity, and the brake lever is only applied when the carp is making for cover.

I know no reel on the market which is so ideal for angling for carp over ten pounds in weight, fish which fight with power and determination.

There have been times when I have been carping in heavily-weeded water (not Thorney) when I have used Alasticum wire for my traces; but I do not consider that this is very satisfactory, for the fish has not much chance and the odds are too much in favour of the angler. In a recent book I have read, this wire is recommended for carp fishing and certainly in a pool where there are tough old lilies and underwater obstructions it may be your only chance of landing your fish. Alasticum wire is used for salmon traces, so I do not think it should be completely barred from the carp angler's outfit.

I would say, however, that a large reel is essential, and your rod should be of the best; a pedigree rod in every way.

In my own pool at Thorney I find that a line with a ten-pound breaking strain fits my purposes, and I usually have a well-tempered salmon-hook attached to stout nylon which is tied direct to the line; or better still, if I am fishing floating bread, the hook is tied direct to the greased line. Eyed hooks are essential for this purpose.

When fishing on the bottom with a lob worm, however, I sometimes use a cast of stout gut or nylon, with one SG shot sixteen inches from the hook. This is, of course, a form of float-ledgering. Some carp fishers never use a float – indeed, it is not really necessary – but, as I have intimated, I cannot get full enjoyment out of fishing unless I have one to look at from time to time.

Hitherto I have confined all my observations to my experiences at Thorney Pond, but I hope later to tell of my adventures elsewhere, not only in my quest for carp but for salmon and trout as well.

In Thorney, should I get a run from a big fish and land him, I do not as a rule have another bite for at least an hour. The scrimmage which follows the hooking of one of these big fish scares everything else for many yards around. And should I have the misfortune to lose one, I usually pack up my tackle.

At the beginning of September, 1947, at the tail end of that superb and memorable summer, I hooked a fish one night in Thorney which pulled with such power, even against my reel, that he shot fifty yards across the pond. I simply dared not touch the brake, he was travelling at such a pace (a 'running' carp has been found to travel at over forty miles an hour).

He took me straight into a tangle of sweet briar which grows down into the water in the east corner, a thicket which had escaped my bagging hook during the summer. There he broke me at leisure and appropriated at least seven feet of line. I often wonder what happens to fish which have been firmly hooked and broken free. I have never caught a carp with a hook in its mouth, yet I lose four or five good fish every season in Thorney Pond.

CHAPTER V

FLOAT, HOOK, LINE, AND SINKER

To speak of 'floats' to a fly fisherman is positively indecent; to the all round angler, who enjoys so-called 'coarse' fishing as well as fly fishing, floats are of immense importance. They contribute greatly to the joys of days and nights by pool, stream, or river; they rest easily on the eye as well as on water. Though, as that great fisherman Sheringham observed, they are more pleasing in their disappearance than in their appearance. Your true dedicated piscator pays as much attention to his floats (or 'bobs' as they are called in USA) as the fly fisherman to his flies. There are some floats which, from their very beginning, fail to give confidence. Their bodies are not stream-lined, some are too fat, some too thin, some sit in the water in a cannot-careless attitude. Others seem alert and expectant, riding the water as though they were alive and capable of spying into the depths, as keen as a kingfisher.

When I was a small boy one could buy wooden 'fishing bats' – two pieces of wood joined by two wires top and bottom, round which, hemmed in by the wooden sides, was line, gut, hook, float, and sinker, all ready to be unwound and attached to the rod. No nonsense about selecting hook or float or strength of gut (for real catgut it was in those days): the youthful angler could set about his business with the minimum of delay. In later years, however, the choosing of a float was a thing to contemplate with gravity and with the weight of experience. The pied quill of a porcupine gave confidence – it had a slim dart-like appearance, yet one missed the bulb of cork – brightly coloured, red, green or white. Like a miniature painted buoy the cork rode the waves, giving the heart of a small boy a thrill each time it lifted to the ripples. And on still days, when the scarlet 'bob' nestled motionless among the lily pads like a brooding bird, even then it gave hope and promise. The single slender quill, with its red rubber band which held the line, was never quite the favourite among my collection for, make no mistake, I collected fishing floats like some boys collected stamps – I had a box full.

There was one which was my favourite. It was a quill, slender and eager, and near its tip a small green and white cork bulb, little bigger than a large raddish. This was always used when fishing for the hog-backed perch which dwelt in the forest of lily roots by a favourite venue we called the Long Log.

This tree, of some size and antiquity, had fallen headlong into the pond years before. Long since, its limbs had decayed away, but it was supported in a horizontal position by some invisible under-water arm which was embedded in the mud. Small boys, walking or crawling along its trunk, had worn the surface quite flat, so flat indeed that green moss grew there. I would crawl along the log to the end and, peering down between the cracks in the lily pads, I could see the bottom of the pond some four feet below. I would drop a worm down into the amber depths and watch its wriggling descent; it took quite a considerable time to reach the bottom. Once there it would writhe and curl until a dark banded shadow would detach itself from other shadows and the worm disappeared in a cloud of mud.

Like a wise hunter who feeds the wild duck onto his pond and refrains from shooting for several weeks, so I fed the perch from the long log until as soon as they felt the vibration of my weight on the log they would be waiting and expectant for the bonanza, from above, swivelling their goggle eye upwards. Then came the day when the worm descended – this time with the deadly, treacherous, barb embedded. The little green and white cork did not linger long between the flat plates of the water lilies, it bobbed then tilted and ran under – the water becoming blurred as the fish went off with the worm. In this way, I usually came home with five or six fish, five or six inches in length, and occasionally one really big fellow with a hump as big as that on a wild boar and a vicious fan of spines bristling on his back – scarlet of fin, glorious to behold and very good to eat, for all the fish I caught we ate, even the little minnows and sticklebacks from the stream; they tasted decidedly muddy.

Another favourite float was a *Fishing Gazette* pike float. This was white with a green base, a portly and important float which rode the water with confidence and seemed at home in the ripples on a wild winter's day as a mallard duck riding the white horses. This bulb of cork was slit, if I remember right, down one side; in this slit you placed your line, holding it in place with a wooden peg. It was a real 'winter' float and looked it, capable of riding out a brisk nor'easter on the reservoir. The principle joy of float fishing is the way different species of fish betray their interest in the bait. The perch bite rejoices the heart of every small country-loving boy. It is an exquisitely prolonged affair affording the youthful piscator a minute or so of tingling excitement and delicious anticipation.

First there may be a slight curtsey among the lily pads, then after an appropriate pause, the quill tip tilts and slides away at an angle until it disappears altogether in the depths. A tench, as everyone knows, has quite a different effect on a float. The watching angler sees the quill lift slightly and then lie flat on its back. This indicates the customer has taken hold of the bait and lifted it upwards from the bottom. One must then be patient and wait until once more the quill is upright and gliding along like the periscope of a submarine.

One hot summer morning in June will always remain in my memory. There was a reservoir not far from my home which was originally constructed to feed the Grand Junction Canal. I awoke at 5 – it was cuckoo time, and that early morning was full of splendour, nobody yet astir, only the cats coming home, slinking and crouching in the quiet fashion these animals have when met with on their wanderings far from the hearth. I found my pitch by a giant willow, whose red roots could be seen like scarlet fingers in the deep olive shade. A mist lay on the water – swallows arrowed by singing as they went – one of the few birds which sing on the wing, a joyous bubbling praise to such a morning. My quill was soon out riding the still water, and as the mist began to draw upwards with the rising of the sun, this quill swooned into a horizontal position and I knew I had a customer. I let it lie motionless than saw it draw slowly away, not yet submerging. I struck and my little rod gave a dangerous bend – I was into one of the fabulous giant tench which dwelt there. I played the fish carefully for ten minutes, for I had fine tackle, but at last I drew it into the waiting net – a handsome tench of over five pounds. The lines of a tench are somehow very attractive, and I have often wished I was a carver of wood so that I could make a panel in some soft white wood showing a bas-relief of the rounded fins and small soft scales, for the tench is nearer the game fish – trout and salmon – than the coarser-scaled species.

As for the bite of roach and bream, the float steams off with barely a preliminary bob.

A barbel bite I cannot describe as I have never fished for them, they are, so I understand, doughty fighters, as are big carp, but inedible. I have had a long experience of carp bites – sometimes they can be exasperating – the quill may give a slight nod or quiver and this may go on for some time before the fish begins to run. The bite of stickleback and minnow is not to be dismissed as trivial. There is a lively bobbing of the float if a slender quill is used followed by quick darting runs.

How tame is the method of fishing without a float! It is difficult to see the line and anglers resort to bells and electric alarms to tell them when a customer has arrived.

I have fished at Redmire, the famous carp water, from which the record fish has been taken, with floatless lines; indeed your professional carp catcher rarely uses a float, the line is placed in an electrical device, originally devised by my friend Richard Walker who was, I suppose, one of the greatest all round fishermen of this century.

As most of big carp feed in the dark hours such devices were necessary but the shock of hearing the sudden buzz from the rod rest when one is in a deep sleep is not to be recommended for those with dodgy hearts. I must confess I know little of seafishing from the shore. I have many times watched and wondered at the solitary figure with his huge rod on its rest complete with little bell which tells him a fish has taken his bait.

Strange to say, I have never once seen a shore fisherman catch anything but weed and crabs. Those I have talked to tell me that it is not often they catch anything worthwhile. Yet a friend of mine, a retired policeman, who lives close to the desolate Lincolnshire coast is a keen cod fisher, setting his lines as a gamekeeper sets his snares and visiting his trap lines at the right state of the tides, night or day, before gulls and crows, and even foxes, can steal the results of his labours. He tells me he nearly always comes home with a 'flask' full of prime cod. He is a true angler, eating what he catches, as I do. Perch from a clear lake or pool are quite delicious and not over-boney, the flesh being a slight bluish tint. Even roach are edible, so are carp whose flesh is slightly golden if the fish came from a gravelly pool.

CHAPTER VI

FISHERMAN ALL

Come to think of it, what a pleasant way it is to spend a summer day beside a pool watching your float! The eye can wander a little to take in the gauzy dance of revolving silver beetles, gnats, and dragon flies, the antics of infant moorhens being fed by the parents, who offer them titbits at the points of their sealing wax red-plated bills, never putting the food directly into the infant's mouth but allowing it to *take* it from the bill tip. Coots also have this habit, as do gulls. What a dreamy world it is, on a hot day in the willow's shade, hearing the bicycle-horn notes of coot which has such a truly watery sound about it. Maybe, too, a blue streak will flash by as a kingfisher heads for its nesting site – a sudden dart of blue lightning which comes and goes so quickly one wonders if one dreamt it.

I suppose that next to a perch bite the most exciting is that of a pike. The float is larger and visible from a distance. If a live bait is attached it is always on the move, curtseying with each movement of the bait. When the pike strikes it usually does so with no nonsense – the float gives a violent dive and disappears for good but you must bide your time before you strike for the pike will have the bait crossways in its ugly jaws and you can easily pull it away from him. Many people like pike to eat but I have never found a way to dissect the flesh from the needle-like bones though I have a faint recollection of pike fish-cakes during the last war which were quite tolerable. It really needs a Frenchman or Frenchwoman to cook coarse fish. I have had roach cooked by a Frenchwoman which was quite delicious, and this reminds me that when I studied art in Paris before the war I used to watch the anglers on the Seine with their long pale roach poles. They caught little fish too which I presume were taken home to madame.

The fishermen of Paris were certainly more successful, apparently than those solitary sea fishermen casting out into the breakers on the bleak Norfolk coast. Match fishing has never been appealing to me – possibly because money is involved with sweepstakes between members – different indeed to the pleasure fishermen. Match fishermen freely admit to this – the lone angler, watching his float, is indeed fishing for pleasure and not for monetary gain.

When I was a boy we constructed a pond and stream below the croquet lawn. This was fed by a constant spring which never failed even in the hottest and most prolonged summer. We put some perch into this stream and after a little while they became absurdly tame, coming to take worms from our fingers. It was an extraordinary sensation to dangle a worm in the water and to have it snatched away as violently as a dog snaps at a biscuit. Unfortunately, this stream was shallow, as was the pond, and marauding herons finished off the fish.

Once a heron begins raiding fish ponds it becomes like a rogue tiger – it will have every fish out of an ornamental pond over a wide area. I was once plagued by such a bird. It became wily, coming on moonlight raids to raid a garden pond close to my house. Time and again I fired a gun under his tail to dissuade him from visiting me but to no avail. Eventually I had to shoot him for he speared the prime golden orfe in my pond and left it on the lawn as it was too big for even his capacious gullet. We plucked and roasted him for supper and excellent he was – no small wonder the heron was a medieval dish. One would have thought that with a fish diet it would have tasted 'fishy' but not so. It went hard, however, to have to execute a fellow angler.

That is why I dislike killing spiders for they are, in a sense, of the brotherhood of fishermen. They spread their nets and wait with as much patience as your dedicted carp catcher.

I like to observe the cunning little hunter concealed high in one corner with his net, so cunningly woven before him so that the first tremor on the line signals a customer. And with what speed they race across to this struggling victim!

Of course, the kingfisher, too is, of the brotherhood and even, would you believe it? the common wren which, so I was told by a man at the Bibury trout farm, were always sneaking the tiny fingerling trout in the spawning beds. Whether this is the habit of the Bibury wrens only I do not know – perhaps, like the tits, they have learnt a new way of obtaining food.

Speaking of Bibury reminds me of how I remember that enchanting village long before the war when there was no line of cars along the wall by the Swan. From the bridge opposite that celebrated hostelry one could look down on the lusty speckled backs of trout among the waving green weed.

It was below this bridge I hooked a goodly trout one Bank Holiday Monday and the battle was observed by rows of gaping holidaymakers lining the bridge. The fish weeded me and I had to go into the Colne to free and net it. I had it for dinner that night at the Swan.

A village which I consider as attractive and far less well known than Bibury is the next village up the stream which meanders down that lovely valley. Ablington was the home of the author of *A Cotswold Village*. One summer afternoon I stood on the bridge at Ablington and watched a dipper busy in the stream. This was a long while since and I doubt if there are any dippers there now – in any case it is an uncommon visitor to Gloucestershire. I knew no finer trees – ash, oak and elm, than those which grew up the valley of the Colne. They are immense – the soil must suit them. As for the stream itself it has much of the charm of Test and Itchen, though perhaps does not have such big trout.

Living as I do in the dull Midlands where no stream runs sweet, pure and clear, those chalk streams are a sheer delight. I suppose the loveliest of all is the Test, though I have never fished it, not because I did not once have the opportunity, but because I am not a skilled fly fisher and this stream is rightly for the elite angler. To mention carp or roach in that part of the world would put you beyond the pale. Viscount Grey had a fishing cottage on the Itchen where he spent some of the happiest hours of his life away from the dreary city and the political scene. He writes beautifully of it in his book and I could not help wondering why a man with such intellect and sense of what is beautiful in the world should have spent so much of his life cooped up in London. He did the writer W.H. Hudson a good turn when he let that great man stay there. Hudson describes the peace and beauty of summer days in that valley of paradise.

CHAPTER VII

HARPER'S BROOK

There is a stream at the bottom of our village which is called Harper's Brook. Who Harper was I cannot discover; maybe he was a seventeenth century miller on the stream for there were two mills on this one short stretch of some five or six miles before it joins the Nene. It serves as a drain for all the surrounding hilly fields and in times of flood causes much havoc and excitement. The lower half of the village goes under, hen and pheasant coops float about, sand bags are put at cottage doors, and the whole aspect of the village is completely changed by a great shiny lake which envelopes the lawns and gardens of the Rectory and sets pigs swimming in their pens, thus disproving the story that if a pig swims it cuts its own throat with its front feet.

It has at least two pairs of resident kingfishers and these occasionally visit my own garden pond where they catch minnows and beat them insensibly on the moss green seal fountain. At the far end of the village stands the old mill house now occupied by a charming lady of title. She has a large family of ducks and geese and many wild mallard. She moves among them at feeding time as though she herself was a feathered being, and they regard her as one. Every afternoon, precisely at 2.30, she emerges from the mill with a bucket of grain. Rows of eager beaks await her and from Harper's Brook there comes hurrying thirty or forty wild mallard who come scrambling to join the feast. Collared doves, too, muscle in. The feast is quickly over, away troop the ducks in waddling line back to the stream – the geese sit down with intucked bills and sleepy pale membranes are drawn like little blinds over their observant eyes – all are replete and satisfied. Once I observed the waiting mob indigently clamouring for their benefactor. The master goose strode up to the mill house door loudly demanding his dinner. The lady was having an afternoon nap so was late in distributing the bounty.

I have reason to believe it was one of her semi-wild mallard ducks which came, in the spring of 1986, and made a nest in the periwinkles by my garden pond six feet from my sitting room window. She hatched twelve lusty babies. She came four weeks later and laid again in the same nest and brought off another dozen striped darlings. Then she paraded round the pond, brooding them at night on the bank. But she did not tarry long, next morning she took them off down the meadow to Harper's Brook. Perils awaited them there, however; a mink had been seen, and some of the ducks at the mill had been killed and no doubt this brute helped himself to those balls of green and yellow down. However, the mink hounds came one steamy June day and killed the mink which, rumour had it, was as big as a large cat.

Standing on the old stone bridge the other day and looking over at the brown stream where the minnow shoals were spawning, I began to think about this little stream, how it has run down the centuries way back into the mists of time. Trees die, as does all life, but this bright water runs eternally, truly as old as the hills. The route of Harper's Brook runs by, little changed since the great forest of Rockingham covered all this part of the country – it must have been running when wild boars roamed and even wolves and bears. Just *when* did it first come to life and movement? – an intriguing thought indeed!

Like so many midland streams it has a charm all its own with its pools and shillets – it flows through pleasant buttercup meadows until it reaches the village and its mill, then on down the valley to Lowick with its fine church and through a little wood, where the reeds grow high and reed warblers churr in summer, and on to the old mill pool which is roofed with the flat plates of water lilies.

Then on, under the main road to join the slow moving Nene which winds its way to the sea. A giant pike dwells in the mill pool at Lowick – some say it is as long as a gate post. Its holt is under the flat lily pads – I have seen his green nose like a giant's shoe, peeping from under the lily leaf. There was also a two pound brown trout hovering in the mill stream – obviously one of those I put in Harper's Brook some years before.

A small boy, fishing for sticklebacks by a willow root downstream had the catch of his life. His float went under for he had a two pound brownie on the other end. He landed it without a net – some feat indeed – and I'll wager he will remember that fish for the rest of his life. I know that spot well. A large willow root forms a sort of cave just by the footbridge from whence I have taken a nice bright dace or two. It was there that the hounds were successful in 'chopping' the giant mink.

Unlike ponds which, in the process of time, silt up and are drained, the stream flows on and therefore has a superior charm. Yet I have always had a great liking for ponds of whatever size. Even the small field pond (and there are not many left now) hold a mystery. There was one such pond not more that fifty yards long by thirty wide which provided me with a great surprise on a recent ramble. It was grown round with thick thorn bushes; indeed every field pond was hedged with bird-sown trees and sloe, and on that sunny September afternoon I stood behind a palisade of flowery willow herb studying the peat brown water. The pond must have been of considerable depth for at its western end the water was dark and fallen branches, just visible in the low rays of the sun, showed it was ten or twelve feet deep in that spot. At the opposite end, however, it was no more than three feet deep. Hanging there, with its shadow on the floor of the pond, was a gigantic common carp – its broad netted back clearly visible – a fish well into double figures. It is not easy to judge the size and weight of a big fish under water – it is invariably larger than it appears due to the refraction of the light. That carp must have been well over twenty pounds. I was intrigued, and enquired of my friend the farmer on whose land the pond lay; he was unable to tell me how the fish got into the pond.

Sometimes the eggs may be carried by the legs of waterfowl – heron and moorhen, but to find such a gigantic fish in such a small and remote pond posed a puzzle which takes some explanation.

Wild duck could easily carry fish eggs on their plumage or paddles. When my mallard duck nested by my pond in the spring of '86 she had to leave her eggs night and morning to go and feed for the mallard drake takes no part in the rearing of the family. But one bright morning her mate appeared, standing just outside my sitting room window on the margin of the pond, his chestnut breast puffed out, his neck and head glittering with wonderful blue-green and purple lights. She came creeping from her nest in the periwinkles and, going up to him, sat down quacking. After a few minute's conversation the lord and master gave himself a shake and flew away and she crept back to her nest in the shadow of the periwinkles.

During the breeding season the drakes go off together for a 'jolly' with the boys on the local reservoirs, different indeed from the red-necked phalarope. There the female lays the eggs and leaves the rearing of the family to the male.

CHAPTER VIII

AN IDLE INTERLUDE

The coarse-fisher, that much despised follower of the craft, has one trenchant argument with which he can confuse the purist: he can learn so much more about the different habits of various species, note their mannerisms and vary his tactics to suit each individual fish. You, being a fly-fisher, have only trout and grayling to watch, and, if you are a rich man, salmon. The coarse-fisher can mark the way the roach shoals swim close under the surface on a warm summer day. Whether in a pool or a river these dainty fish are ever on the move; they huddle like a flock of sheep, keeping all together; each shoal seems to have some appointment it must keep, or some ever-present fear of a pursuer.

Sitting on the bank of the river under the shady slender leaves of the willows, it is pleasant to watch the roach. It is the heat of noon, the June sun blazes down, and behind us, among the golden lakes of buttercups, the red cattle are running with upraised tails. They have been driven from the shallows at the bend of the river by a single humming insect no bigger than a bee. Yet what terror does the bot-fly spread among those ruminating ranks! What a fierce pain he must be able to inflict on those thick red hides, for the apprehensive beasts behave as if all the fiends were after them.

We, fortunate idle men, can sit at ease in the green coolness of this tree, and discuss at leisure the contents of our food-bags and perhaps a bottle of mature beer, packed so daintily and lovingly by our long-suffering wives. Beer, spring onions, and cheese, go well with coarse fishing. For my part I have a liking for plebeian foods. Winkles I like, and mussels, and such things as pigs' trotters and chitterlings do not come amiss. Such fare would not do for you, perhaps, a fly-fisher of the South.

We have been angling all the morning, since sunrise.

To be a successful river fisherman you must be well acquainted with the water; a stranger coming here might angle for a week and only get a few small perch and eels.

Shimmering in the heat haze is Bredon Hill, made famous by the charming poem of that title. Truly today it is 'Summertime on Bredon'. In the water-meadows over the river they are cutting the hay; all morning the machine has been crawling round and round, and the stutter of the tractor and clatter of the machine has filled the ear with a drowsy murmur. It is a pity the horse is going out of agriculture, for we have gained nothing from the advent of the petrol engine, whatever men may say. It is a destroyer of peace. Your true coarse-fisher has no use for speed – it is the very antithesis of what he considers a right and proper mode of life. The only advantage may be that he can perhaps get to his fishing grounds with greater ease and spend a longer day than would be the case if he had to catch a train.

But in this flaming noon even the tractor is silent and the haymakers have sought the shade of the willows over there on the river bank. Sensible fellows!

But we were talking just now of fish. If you watch the sunlit water opposite it will not be long before you see something of interest. Small flies are jigging in the shade of our tree, marionettes pulled up and down by invisible threads. Rotifers are skating figures of eights on the cool, green-shadowed water; they appear to me like minute silver racing cars such as one sees at fairs. (But then, if you are a fly-fisher, you probably never go to fairs.)

Here come the roach, just as I told you they would. First a couple of lusty fish: they must be well over the pound mark, and one I swear is nearer two. After them stream the main body. They go by ceaselessly, their golden eyes fixed and apprehensive. Unlike a bird or an animal, fishes ever seem to be wide awake and slightly horrified, yet I seem to recollect observing a perch questing the piles of my boat house at Thorney Pond at home who had a most contented, inquiring look in his big swivelling eye.

There, the last roach has passed by, but in ten minutes or so they will be coming back, the big ones still leading. It is, I think, pure joy of swimming that makes the roach such rovers. They must have continual exercise.

They have gone again, and the zittering chatter of a sedge warbler in the reeds close by is the only thing that claims our attention. Have you noticed, I wonder, how the song of these little tripeds short-tailed birds, with their big heads, seems to be full of river talk? They are shy too, and one rarely sees the songster; only the quiver of a reed or a glimpse of a small brown creature with shortish wings is vouchsafed to you. Wherever you find sedge warblers in June, there also will the cuckoo be. Even now I hear one over the meadows yonder. He is a long way off, and I can hear only the second note, tolling like a bell. Sedge warblers are favourite victims of the cuckoo; frequently the great greedy offspring, bulging in the nest like a fat woman confined in a pair of undersized corsets, will end up by falling into the river underneath. I have found many drowned young cuckoos in my idle fisherman's ramblings.

Where the scarlet fingers of the willow roots feel down into the water just below us, I observe a movement. Yes, it is a perch – in fact, several small perch.

I seem to remember that I talked with bitterness and scorn of this fish earlier on. Do not misunderstand me. I like the perch; he is a pretty bold-biting fish, as old Izaak says, and on the table, if properly cooked, your river perch can equal a trout – indeed I have known occasions when it has surpassed that spotted aristocrat in flavour.

Too many people have tasted pond perch to believe that the species can ever be good to eat. If it was not too hot I would put on a small hook, a number ten maybe, and with one of those red worms which are cool and snug in yonder tin I would angle for these fish we see at this moment and, having caught a kettle full, I would light a fire and cook them and you should tell whether or no I am making a false statement.

The flesh is bluish, firm, and comparatively boneless. That raises another point about eating coarse fish (as we are eating at the moment, it will be, methinks, a suitable topic of conversation).

Many people have no idea of how to eat fish; even a herring defeats them completely. They do not know its anatomy. Watch your average non-fisherman (and sometimes even, alas, skilled fisherman!), how he attacks a cooked fish. In nine cases out of ten he will have it parallel with him on the plate. He takes his knife and fork, digs the fork into the shoulder and tries to cut slices from it with the knife as if it were a piece of prime steak. Result – a grisly mess of flesh and needle-like bones. One might as well eat a pincushion.

If it is not too much effort, pass me the creel by your elbow, and I will demonstrate how you should eat one of those roach you caught at sunrise.

There, I have him on the plate before us. Notice that I turn him so that his tail is towards me and his head facing the river where six hours ago he was disporting himself. You will notice the median line, that neat line which runs down his side, that neat stitching which mother Nature employs in finishing her finny products.

See, I stick the fork into the head and with the knife I gently cut along the line. Actually, as this fish is raw, I cannot demonstrate the action to a nicety, but you must imagine that the flesh is flaky, white and soft.

Now, with a gentle motion, I push the blade *sideways* and *backwards* in the same direction as the lie of the bones. The fillet comes away with ease, practically without a bone. Now turn it over and serve the other side the same. This leaves us the flesh covering the ribs. These are the bones which confuse and disgust the non-expert.

Turn the fish on his back now and press him apart, press with the knife-blade on the bones next to the backbone. *Pin* the bones to the plate. Now turn the fork at right angles, like a rake, and pull the flesh away from the immovable bones. Serve each side the same, and there you have good meat such as Izaak would have delighted in – and not a bone in any of it.

I quite agree that a biggish bone in the throat can cause you much discomfort and ruin your day.

The perch is even the more easy to deal with as his back steaks are devoid of bones.

River fish are always better to eat than those from ponds, but I would have you come with me one day to Thorney Pond and catch one of my carp. Having drawn my fish on to the bank, and supper time being arrived, I wrap him in wet newspaper or even moss and leaves, binding him, in the latter case, with a slender briar.

My camp fire having died to a mass of embers, I scrape the latter aside and place my carp, wrapped in its winding sheet, among them.

In twelve minutes or so he will be done. I take him out, unwrap his shroud (which is now almost burnt through), and as I peel these wrappings apart the skin comes with it and there is my fish cooked as well as if by a Savoy chef.

I will not say that he is as good as a river perch, or even a pond perch, but he is very good and a worthy meal for a hungry fisherman.

That perch down there has seen something in the red rootlets. His back fins are raised as a dog raises the bristles on its back. He has certainly seen something: and he is like a cat about to spring on a mouse. There...he springs, a lightning dart forward, and has backed away with fins working, making a round mouth. Fins are a great tell-tale. One day I will show you a pike waiting to make a kill. He will lie motionless, his nose perhaps protruding from a parasol of weeds. his fins are still, he appears a stuffed fish. But let some small roachling come his way and observe those fins! They start to winnow quickly, a lovely motion. The tips curl with the water-pressure, and he moves slowly round, *aiming* himself at the fish. The actual take is so rapid that the eye cannot follow it.

I often think that it would be fun to watch one of my Thorney carp take a worm. The lightning action must be similar, for one's first warning is usually the scream of the reel. Even the action of a carp taking floating bread is very rapid. There is not often a gentle 'suck in'. The fish swims slowly round, gets wind of the bread, and approaches gently. Then there is a swirl, a blurred vision of a broad-netted back, and he is gone and sometimes your line as well.

We can learn much by sitting still on a summer's day under a willow. Imagine fly-fishing in this heat! The idea is positively indecent!

I would draw your attention to another matter, as at the moment no fish are moving in our natural aquarium.

Out in the sunlight there is a clump of bluish rod-like reeds; *Juncus Communis* is the name, if you wish to know it. You don't? – well, then, I will not weary you with the Latin derivation, and it is too hot anyway. See how they seem to be alive, their needle tips wagging though there is no breeze; see how they lean away from the slow current. Possibly, as you are a fly-fisher and have no eyes or ears for these things, you have not been aware (as I have) of a slight masticating sound which has been going on for some moments. Somebody else is having his luncheon, too. It is a water-vole. He sits on his raft of laid reed and holds a juicy section of stalk in his hands as a squirrel holds a nut. He eats quickly, the stalk growing shorter as it rises into the cutting teeth. He enjoys his river salad, does the water-vole. The action is rapid, and he shifts his little hands with skilful speed.

There are some rivers where you may lure big cannibal trout with water-voles, but it is a cruel practice because it necessitates killing the vole first with a well-aimed air gun pellet. The body is 'spun' as you would a spoon. Only very big trout will take it, and often a pike will be there first.

You cannot see the vole? – why, man, you must be blind! But then you are a fly-fisher.... I forgot. Anyway, you cannot see him now because he has gone downstairs to his underwater parlour entrance. That widening ring denotes his departure; it is *not* caused by a rising fish.

The roach are coming back. You wish to try and catch one? What a restless fellow you are! We are not well placed just here – if we were on a bridge it might be possible.

Sit still and watch. Hullo! – the roach seem more lethargic. They swim more slowly; some turn about end-on to us, including the big fellow which I would fain have in my basket. You can see his breadth of back.

You think there must be a pike lurking under the water-voles's platform? No, you are wrong. The roach at last have decided to take a noon-day nap. They stand about in a dreamy way and most are rising up almost touching the surface of the water with their backs, just like my Thorney carp which I have told you of.

The water must be very warm out there. I do not think that even Izaak, or Trent otter, or Hugh Sheringham, could tempt one of those fish to look at anything, for they are sun-bathing. Most fish glory in it, but I have not known tench sunning to the same extent. They will do so, however, on very hot days at Thorney, for I have seen them under the lily pads, blowing their pale mouths at me.

How queer these fish appear, dotted about before us. Some are facing us, others are tail-on, some lie lengthwise – all motionless....

What a splash! The whole surface of the river boils for a moment, and there is not a fish to be seen. A pike? No. You may not have noticed, as I did, that house martin sweep by, half-screened by the hanging willow leaves. It was the bird that put them down: they are terrified of anything flying overhead.

You ask the reason? Really, the fly-fisher....! Most fish are scared of movement over their heads because, all down the ages, they have been preyed upon by kingfishers and possibly (away back in time) fish-eating hawks. A poor life you say? Maybe; terror lurking in the sky, terror lurking in the reed bed, terror lurking even in the appetising red brandling sprawling on the river sand. Yet they enjoy this hour as much perhaps, in their way, as I am enjoying mine.

Perhaps when the sun has gone and there descends the healing peace of evening on this delectable river, we will try a little farther down beyond this willow for that big roach. I shall put on a large ball of paste, as big as a marble, and pretend to be a clump of meadow sweet.

That reminds me.... Meadow sweet, another delight for the river angler! What garden flower has so sweet a perfume as this ivory-bloomed, soft-leaved river plant? And across the river there is a wild rose bush with the first pink buds upon it. You had not noticed it? Of all the roses, wild or tame, give me the sweetbriar roses in bud, those tender pink-tipped pointed bulbs of rolled petals. To see them gives me unutterable delight, and yet they make me sad for I know that summer is at its prime. But that is foolish talk. No season of the year is without its charm and own peculiar beauty, though the summer, high summer, is the cream of the year.

I see you are putting away your pipe, that you shoot covert glances at the willow trunk against which our slender fishing wands are idly propped. Perhaps you are wishing yourself by the side of Test; or Kennet, maybe? They are wondrously beautiful rivers, and I would not mind a day there myself just now. All the same, it is 'summertime on Bredon', and if you wish to be up and doing – very

Perhaps you are wishing yourself by the side of Test; of Kennet, maybe? They are wondrously beautiful rivers.

well.... Some people must be wagtails I suppose. I prefer to keep my tail still and sit upon it under the willow here. In fact, (if you do not mind) I will take a little nap. I see that the roach are taking up station again out there.

If you like to wander down the bank I will meet you later, and we will quaff a nut-brown pint together at Twyning Fleet.

CHAPTER IX

THE TEMPLE POOL

R.W., my fellow carp addict of the magic hat, with whom the reader has already made a nodding acquaintance earlier in these pages, has met his Waterloo. This melancholy intelligence reached me only last week.

Before I tell you how this came about, let me say that R.W. is a very worthy disciple of Izaak Walton, and possesses great skill. Carp are, as with me, his grand passion, and I suppose he knows more about this species than any man in England, for his experience has been gained in a wide and varied field and by divers waters.

He has a deep and weedy clay pit near his house where lately, in his company, I did battle with several doughty warriors and managed to bring to bank, after stern and midnight struggles, four carp ranging from eight and a half pounds to ten pounds two ounces.

These fish are, however, small beer compared with what R.W. and I saw in another pool which is the subject of this chapter.

In the small pool of his I was, on two occasions, thoroughly threshed and trounced by unseen giants, and in consequence (let me make a clean breast of it) I forsook stout nylon and got R.W. to make up for me a trace of banjo wire. I shudder even now to think that I descended so low, but I was driven to desperate action. The pond is full of old bedsteads and discarded bicycles. There was some excuse for this regrettable lapse. And when next my floating bread was seized by an unseen leviathan, I won through by sheer strength of tackle. Even then it got me round a bedstead in the darkness and, had I been using gut or nylon, I should have been served in different fashion.

I shudder even now when I remember how that ten-pounder took me. I was alone, R.W. had gone home to raid the pantry for further bread supplies, and it was a very dark night; moreover, the bank was steep and slippery, and the water ten feet deep close to the bank.

It was so dark that when I at last staggered up the bank with some obscure and heavy weight in my net I did not know if I had captured a carp or ten pounds of wet weed.

What a delightful holiday that was, and how patient his wife, a model for all fishermen's wives! Later I must pay tribute to these noble women, but first I will tell of how R.W. and I fared at the Temple Pool, where later he was to meet his match.

This water, which was six miles or so from R.W.'s house, was the carp-fisher's dream. It belonged to an old and titled family living in Bedfordshire and was of great beauty. Strictly private, well-keepered, tenanted by enormous carp, it appeared at first sight a 'piece of cake', as the saying is.

Actually there were two pools, one below the other. The upper lake before the mansion contained rainbow trout, the lower, carp, roach, and a few escaped rainbows from the lake above. It was a remarkably beautiful water, fringed with shrubberies and many trees, through which meandered a leaf-strewn narrow path. Between the pools was a Grecian temple erected in the eighteenth century by our host's ancestors, hence the name.

We first went over for a reconnaissance, for no good carp-fisher ever begins operations without some sort of 'recce'.

The August day was sublime with a hot sun and the still airs misty with cruising flies. No more propitious hour could have been vouchsafed to us for our preliminary inspection.

This lower pool was not wide, not more than thirty to forty yards across, but very long. It had been formed by damming a biggish brook, and the dam was at the eastern end. There the water was fairly deep, about six or seven feet. The rest of it was shallow, varying from four to five feet. Out in the centre was a good deal of weed, but not of a vicious nature; it was the woolly underwater species which carp delight in.

My first reaction was that it would be sheer murder to allow two experienced carp-fishers like ourselves to try our skill. The carp seemed absurdly tame; they had evidently never learnt to fear the two-legged animal on the bank, for, as we strolled along the path, they swam about unconcernedly within a yard or so of us. Never had I had the opportunity of observing these fish with such ease, for close in the water was free of weed and fairly clear.

There were the two varieties, mirror and common, and they appeared to range from three- and four-pounders to nine- or ten-pound fish. We had brought some bread with us. This we threw in, and several of the smaller carp swam round and devoured it. I almost thought we had better not come on the morrow of our passion for carp-fishing might be spoilt for life. I should, of course, have known better and given the carp their due; I should have remembered that they are, without doubt, the most cunning and circumspect of all our coarse fish.

Perhaps, I suggested to R.W., it would be better if he left his hat at home, and substituted for it some other less-potent form of headgear.

We walked the length of the lake under the shady trees and smoked a pipe on a fallen log, observing these lovely creatures swimming by or basking out in the middle.

The centre weeds seemed to be heaving with carp, and some lay like logs just under the surface, their porpoise backs showing. It is very hard, as I have said, to tell the size of fish when they are in the water, but I looked for those with small heads and slightly humped backs. These portents usually mean that they are glass-case specimens.

Then R.W.'s pipe nearly fell from his mouth and he clutched my arm. I followed his gaze and we beheld, swimming out from under a weed bed, the two biggest carp I have ever seen. One fish we put at nineteen pounds or so; the other was much larger, well over twenty-six and probably nearer thirty. It was prodigious. When it turned end-on to us it appeared to be as wide as one of those oaken kegs which former agriculturalists took with them to the harvest fields.

We sat for a while gazing in a sort of trance until these two ponderous giants glided away with dignified mien under the weeds.

'My hat!' gasped R.W.

'You'll need it!' I returned, abandoning all thoughts of half-measures.

On the morrow we were at Temple Pool bright and early, but the day was not too good. There was a good deal of cloud, and soon after dawn it began to rain.

R.W. picked his site one hundred yards above the dam; I planted myself twenty yards from it, opposite a small island on which grew yew bushes and six or seven tall trees. There was a swan's hut on the island.

Both of us were using lob worm as bait, intending to try floating bread should the sun come out later. We began fishing soon after sunrise. Both of us had floats and our casts were stout nylon.

R.W. had a run soon after he had put in, and I again thought that it was going to be a bad day for these seemingly uneducated carp, especially when I saw R.W.'s rod bent in an arc – obviously a good fish. After some lively play, during which the fish twice buried itself in the weeds in the middle of the pool, he netted it, a mirror carp of a little over three pounds. I never had a bite.

R.W. had hardly put in again when he had a second run. This from a much large carp. This fish also made a dive for the thick weeds where, after a longish struggle, it managed to get off. Still I had no run, but then I was wearing no Magic Hat so it did not surprise me (or perhaps R.W. is a much better carp-fisher than I, which is a much more probable explanation).

After that there was a long lull. We had breakfast. Some very good carp began to be visible during the morning, patrolling the weed beds, though we saw no signs of the giants.

Having no luck whatever in my pitch, I moved round to the opposite side of the island where I had seen a carp of about fifteen pounds, with a scar on his shoulder, patrolling up and down. But I did no good there either and, rather mystified, I left my rod to fish itself and walked down the path.

By now the sun had come out, and more and more fish emerged from the weed bed and began to swim up and down.

As soon as the water was well warmed, a single cygnet appeared from nowhere, swimming sedately up the lake and pulling at the weeds as he came. I have no love for swans; they are arrogant birds and sometimes are hasty-tempered. This one seemed harmless enough, and beyond a few extraordinary croaks it took no notice of me and continued to up-end his absurd posterior among the weeds, which showed how shallow the water was just there. His activities, however, disturbed the carp, and soon he was routing about in the very weed bed which I believed to hold the two giants. I was correct. In a moment or so they came slowly out, evidently not liking this disturber of their peace. The larger one obligingly swam slowly towards me as I stood half-hidden behind a bole. He came, I suppose, to within ten yards, and I was able to get a splendid view of his proportions. I saw that he was a mirror, a most perfect fish, with a few big scales on his side. In colour he was a rich mahogany, shading to bluish black on the back.

He came slowly along, head on, appearing not unlike an inflated balloon under the water. Then he turned and swam out of sight behind some bushes.

I moved my 'Palakona', which was still hopefully fishing by the island, and changed to floating bread. Meanwhile R.W. had moved up to my old pitch and had put out a worm on ledger and had settled down to catch some roach. Evidently he surmised that chances for carp were gone until evening.

With his light tackle and plenty of ground-bait he began to catch a nice basket, and it amused me a good deal to see him smile seraphically to himself every time he swung a fish in. Many were good fish up to and over the half-pound mark.

Several big carp swam past my floating bread without taking the slightest notice of it; but one common carp of three pounds or so spitefully gulped down a crust which I had thrown in a few feet from my floating lure, and this gave me hope.

But the day wore on and nothing looked at me. In the early afternoon, after lunch, R.W.'s ledger began to run out and, after a struggle, he landed a nice rainbow of about two pounds which had taken the lob. Unfortunately this fish had bolted the worm and had to be killed, otherwise we should have returned him to the upper lake.

Things were now very slack, as it was just past middle day and most of the carp, when they were not disturbed by the swan (who was still up-ending all over our area), lay about sunning. The big chaps had retired again to their weedy fastness.

After tea things began to liven up. I went back to my old pitch and soon after had the first run of the day. Like the others, this fish went straight for the weeds, despite considerable pressure, and I had some trouble before I got him clear and fought it out with him in the clear water in front of the island. This proved to be a lovely common carp of four pounds. Both these carp we had caught were put in the keep net by the dam.

The shades of evening now began to fall, and a breeze stirred the trees overhead, though the pool itself, being so sheltered, was glass-smooth.

R.W. had a succession of runs from carp, all of which he lost in some inexplicable way. They did not seem to be biting boldly. Perhaps the Hat had lost some of its power.

Just after 7 p.m. I had another run, and this time he beat me, plunging about in the weeds from which I had been unable to hold him off. This I think was the best carp I had hooked that day, and must have been in the ten-pound region.

There came another slack time; possibly the disturbance caused by the fight had scared the carp away, for I noticed they were not now swimming opposite to us. Darkness came at last without any further bites.

The two carp we caught we took home and put in R.W.'s pond, in a keep net, and the next day I put them in a sack in the back of the car and motored sixty miles to my home where I put them in my rockery pool. They swam away with fine unconcern, which shows the toughness of the fish. They are very much alive in my rockery pool at this moment.

That night R.W., and I could talk of nothing but the big fish, and I was only too sad that I was leaving on the morrow and would be unable to go again that season.

Evidently these two large carp had their own particular haunt; we never saw them down by the island; they were always near the weed-bed halfway down the lake.

It was a rather difficult place to reach or even to approach with a line, as the trees were fairly thick along the bank, which made casting tricky work. R.W., however, is a person of great resource, and having obtained permission to cut a few openings in the brambles and bushes opposite the weed bed he went again during this last September, hoping to connect with the giant or giants.

The first time he went he fished all night, and he tells me in an interesting letter that after sundown the carp went off feed and did not come on again until after dawn. This could be explained, however, by the fact that the nights were then growing cold and the carp were not moving much during the hours of darkness. He had a nice fish of about eight pounds, but nothing larger.

His next and last visit was a week later, and it was then he met his Waterloo.

On his first visit he had not only cleared the brambles and made an opening with a bagging-hook, but had also taken the precaution of dredging out some sunken wood which lay out from the bank. He arrived at the Temple Pool about 8 a.m., having overslept (he had meant to get there by dawn). He tied a big salmon eyed hook direct to his line and pinched on a SG shot a yard from it. He decided to fish without a float. He baited with a lob worm and managed, by skilful casting, to get it well out not far from the weed bed. He also threw in some broken worms.

Very soon there were signs of carp moving, and the water became 'alive' – bubbles and so forth.

He soon had a run, a fish of twelve pounds, but it was not this but the big one that he was after. At 2 p.m. the two monsters appeared in an open 'lagoon' among the weeds, about twenty yards from his sunken bait.

After a little aimless cruising and sunning, the big chap came nearer and began to glide very slowly over the spot where the worm had sunk. It was an exciting moment for R.W., but the great fish did not seem to be in the mood for taking anything.

Imagine R.W.'s feelings, however, when it began to take an interest. It 'back pedalled' slowly, and then tilted downwards and disappeared from view in a leisurely manner exactly over the spot where the ledger was!

R.W. had coiled three feet of line on the bank, and as he bent down to seize the rod he saw it begin to travel surely out. That was indeed a moment!

It seemed to take an age before the last coil whispered through the rings and he raised the rod point, seeing the droplets of water sliding down the line.

R.W. tells me in his letter that there was then a tremendous underwater disturbance, the whole lake bed seemed to boil, and away went the carp like an express train right down the lake, sending a wave washing on either hand. There followed a terrific battle. Many times it went into the weed bed. But each time hand-lining was efficacious. It is strange how effective this method is when dealing with a weeded fish. One may pull for hours, all day even, with the rod point and your adversary will ignore you; but a steady pull with the hand he cannot abide, and so it was in this case.

At last R.W. had him slowly circling opposite to him, a sure sign of a tiring fish, and before long he could pull it into a gaffing distance. He had the gaff in his hand, but, like the great sportsman he is, he shrank from using it on this fish and all the more credit to him. Instead he took up his salmon landing-net, and after a moment or so the opportunity arrived and he put it under the fish.

But when he tried to lift the vast bulk he was horrified to see it slip over the edge; its weight was so terrific that single-handed he could not drag it out, for he was still holding his rod in his left hand.

Again he brought it in, and this time he got it well inside the net (even then the great tail was hanging out); but, alas, again out went the fish – the line broke at the hook tie....

R.W. sent me the line, and I could see that it was frayed right through with the terrific strain and friction of the battle.

Anglers are always open to gibes when they talk of the 'one that got away', but R.W. swears that this fish was a British record. Having seen the carp, I do not doubt him for a moment. Had there been someone at hand to help with the net that fish would have been landed. As it is – he is still in the Temple Pool, and I hope to challenge him myself this year, hat or no hat.

CHAPTER X

SHREDS AND PATCHES

It is raining again! No, even my enthusiasm is evaporating, and I suggest we seek the ivied gloom of the boat-house. I have never done any good in heavy rain, and by the look of the sky yonder we are going to be prisoners for a little while yet.

This enthusiasm for fishing is a strange thing. We set forth so full of hope to river or pool, and even if the fish will not show themselves interested in our lures, we ply our wands with inextinguishable zeal. But after a while, when noon has passed and gone and we are yet without a bite of any sort, we feel our keenness ebbing away like sands in an egg boiler, and soon we begin to think that there are no fishes to be caught. We no longer regard the water as shielding unseen monsters, and should it begin to rain, even the beauties of the world seem slightly stale.

Why fish will not bite during rain I do not know, unless it is something to do with the amount of oxygen in the water.

After rain it is a different matter: then is frequently a most propitious time, for they emerge to seek what the heavens have brought them, half-drowned flies and washed-in worms. The amount of worms that enter even my small garden pool after a heavy shower of rain is quite astonishing. But these are mere platitudes.

Let us then to the boat-house and pass the time in discussing angling matters, for the next best thing to fishing for fish is talking about them.

We may even see a few perch to liven our discourse: they frequently tour these oaken piles as they will the roots of an old oak, and even during rain I have taken some good fish here. Perch are fond of shadow from tree or bridge, and so, for that matter, are most fish. Trees are ever spreading manna on the waters in the shape of grubs and flies.

It is a pity, you know, that we anglers have the reputation for exaggeration. Some, of course, accuse us roundly of flagrant lying. I grant you that there are some fishermen who exaggerate, but very few. I have lately been turning over in my mind why other sportsmen have not acquired a similar slandered character; fox-hunting men, let us say, or those who shoot. One of the reasons is, I suppose, that in fox-hunting one is seldom alone (unless one is a beginner or a bad rider). It would be pointless to boast of a spectacular run, because so many of one's fellows would immediately know whether or no one were telling the truth. Similarly, in shooting, unless you are a lone hunter or a wild-fowler, it is useless to talk of the sky darkened by grouse or pheasants, or of your gun so hot that you could not hold it, a phenomenon due to the excessive number of shots you had fired. There are other guns on your flanks; you cannot exaggerate. If you are a single-handed shooter and you boast of a big bag of game, the chances are that you will be asked for a brace, and then you will look foolish. The same applies to golf. There may be men who boast of their prowess with the golf club, but there will be a cloud of witnesses. Most of these anglers who do exaggerate are only anxious to share their excitement and pleasure with others.

Fishing is not a sociable sport, any more than wild-fowling is. I hear you murmur something about fishing-matches. I myself have seen a river bank lined with earnest men, sitting within a stone's throw of each other – and an offensive sight it is to me. The match-fisher is not my idea of a true fisherman. What joy a man can find in being one of a row, the object being to catch as many fish as he can in a given time, irrespective of size, I do not know, and the habit of crowding thirty or forty small roach into a miserable keepnet is most reprehensible. Most of the fish will die or become so injured that they will die when they are released.

Some anglers exaggerate because they need to keep their spirits up, and to encourage fellow anglers whom they meet after their sport. This is sometimes necessary and is good for the soul. No man can say that the true angler is an unsociable person; indeed, the pleasure of going over one's battles again, with a tankard in one hand and a pipe in the other, is very attractive. It is always the big fish that get away? – of course it is! by their very strength and girth they smash our tackle and depart, and we can show our shattered tackle as proof. But the unbelievers will only smile and dart sidelong glances at one another. This but adds insult to injury. For the majority of anglers tackle is expensive, especially in these days; it is a grave matter if some hefty tench, carp, salmon, or trout departs with our gear.

I have seen one, glassy-eyed and incoherent, displaying a shattered top joint for all to see, undeniable proof that he had been broken by a big fish. Yet none believed him save his brother anglers. It is monstrous, this disbelief in our veracity.

Instead of taking the poor fellow tenderly by the arm and patting him gently on the back, instead of leading him to a chair and calling for the landlord to fill the flowing bowl, this poor wretch's story was greeted with shouts of ribald laughter.

Yet we anglers who are broken by big fish, even though we lose our tackle, are filled with a certain fearful joy. I would rather be broken by a big fish than catch a hundred roachlings. A man who has been through that experience is treated by his fellow anglers with awe; the matter is discussed with bated breath, as though he had been through some awful experience, almost as if he had returned from the gates of death, or but recently recovered from a dire operation.

If fish never grew beyond half-a-pound in weight, I should give up fishing and leave the sport to the match-fishers.

To return for a moment to the latter. They are, in nearly every case, townsmen, who have become so used to working and taking their pleasures in company that they cannot enjoy their leisure hours without companions. Even fishing-clubs I regard with a shrinking horror.

I well remember fishing a certain pool famous for its weighty carp. The rights belonged to a fishing-club from whom one purchased tickets, but the club only fished their water three or four times a season, as it was in remote country and very inaccessible.

By evil chance I happened to be there on one of these very days, and soon after 10 a.m., when all good carp-fishers are packing up their gear and making home for breakfast (I was so employed), there descended upon that lovely tree-girt water a horde of men, women and children, who had arrived (unbeknown to me) in a fleet of charabancs.

My leafy solitude was broken by loud shouts and laughter, and down the bank they streamed. It was like a Sunday School 'outing'. The women feathered along the bank and spread out rugs and mackintoshes, ginger-beer and other drinks flowed freely, orange peel was thrown into the pond, and I watched with an awful fascination the male members of this gathering setting up their rods. Some attached large globes of lead to the end of lines and hurled them in to plumb the depth, others stamped up and down the banks looking for a pitch, shouting to each other all the time; the children ran hither and thither throwing sticks and stones into the water. Some even made ready to swim.

Needless to say, I took my departure with all haste and returned not again for a week.

There is, of course, the low type of professional fisherman who spreads abroad the big fish story in order that he may lure gold into his pocket. And there is the man who likes to attract attention to himself on the chance of a free drink. It is these people who bring us true anglers into disrepute.

What possible reason is there for a man to spread abroad that he has seen a very big fish? Surely he will keep his secret, so that he may go privily at an early hour and catch it for himself. If you were to tell me that anglers are jealous, then I might agree with you; there would be some grounds for the assertion.

Anglers are more jealous of their particular haunts than any other sportsmen. Sometimes they have good reason to be. It calls for a considerable sense of humour to temper your dismay at finding a fellow fisher ensconced in a spot which you have been assiduously ground-baiting for the last ten days in hope of catching a big fish which you happen to know is there. It is not a pleasant thing to see another man reap what you have sown. Sometimes this is accidental, but there are certain so-called sportsmen who watch from afar, unseen, when you are baiting up a pitch and when you depart they arrive.

The jealousy of fly-fishers is well known. There is a certain type of man who will pick the best spot in a salmon pool and not budge from it – not even threats of physical violence can move him.

I promised just now to say a word in praise of fisherman's wives. Women, as we have observed, do not fish, save a very small minority and they are nearly always fly-fishers. The majority have the home to look after and the children to tend (the female sex works much harder all through life than the male). To get through their day comfortably, meals must be regular and, when cooked, must be eaten. Alas! – as we have shown, your true angler cares not for his stomach when he is after fish; meals are a positive nuisance to him until his angling is done, which may be at any hour of day or night.

Carp-fishers' wives are the most long-suffering of them all. Not only are their menfolk invariably late for meals, but they have the ghastly habit of rising long before dawn and clattering about the house, which makes further sleep out of the question. The woman needs refreshing sleep to carry on with her daily tasks.

Worse still, he will, on occasion, rise in the middle of the night, or come home at one in the morning, an hour when most warm-blooded creatures are deep in slumber. Not only this: there have been occasions when live fish have been found swimming in the bath. This is the last straw, and should be as good grounds for divorce as any.

R.W.'s wife, when she presented her lord and master with a son, returned from hospital to find a sixteen-pound carp disporting in the bath, with R.W. trying to get it out. Yet this wonderful little woman makes no moan; she is resigned, I suppose, and there is nothing she can do about it. She cleans and cooks his catch in spite of the fact that her best empty tins (and not always empty) have been appropriated for worms.

Yet I think most fishermen's wives are lucky. Their men are much better employed by a river's bank than getting up to vicious mischief elsewhere. They are, in the main, steady fellows who love their wives and children dearly and are men of peace. They have never really grown up; they have in them much of the boy and the boy's enthusiasm, and the mothering instinct is aroused.

I believe that this is the reason why not very many anglers of the right sort are bachelors; they are soon hooked. I have known one or two, however, very wary fish, who have remained single, but they are crochety fellows of jealous disposition. Had they been carp they would have grown to a ripe old age and finally be found dead on the banks of the pond where they had lived all their lives.

Railway men, hairdressers, butlers and publicans, and sometimes schoolmasters, make the best type of coarse-fishermen. Retired army people make the best fly-fishers. Their various professions have enabled them to have a certain amount of leisure and also the opportunities for good fishing. In the old days butlers and grooms had wonderful opportunities for fishing in private lakes. Their masters were not interested in coarse fish, and they could usually go whenever they felt inclined. There is no better angling in the whole of Britain (I speak of coarse fish) than that to be found in private lakes on large estates. Nowadays these lakes, which were in most cases made in the eighteenth century, when almost every mansion had its lake or pool, have become derelict and almost unfishable. The cleaning of a lake is a very costly business, and unless it is attended to every ten years a water will soon become quite unfishable, except when it is very deep. There are always trees in its vicinity, and every autumn the leaves add their quota, branches and even whole trees fall in, and it is quite astonishing how even a deep water can soon become shallow. Much silt is brought into the lake by the feed-stream unless measures have been taken to prevent it. This, more than any cause, is the reason why they become useless and shallow.

It is quite easy to prevent silt entering a pool by the erection of tumbling bays and grills. If every spring the fallen timber were dragged out and the accumulation of leaves removed, the life of a lake would be indefinite.

If it were possible for trout to thrive in land-locked waters, much more attention would be paid to this matter; but the average landowner has no use for coarse fish and the water is there purely for ornamental reasons.

CHAPTER XI

RESTLESS RODS

It may have been guessed from what I have so far written that I am a stay-at-home angler, an unadventurous man who finds all his pleasures by, and in the solemn deeps of, Thorney Pond

This, however, is not the case; I am as restless at times as a migratory fish-eating bird, and if circumstances allow I like to wander with my rod and let it lead me into new and pleasant pastures. Change is good for the spirit and broadens one's outlook; also it is good for my rod and me to look upon different scenes.

One of the ways to enjoy life is to make it, if you can, as varied as possible; it is surely the secret of the difficult art of living. Were I a man of great wealth, if tomorrow I should receive word that a kind and unknown benefactor had left me fifty thousand pounds a year (free of income tax), I should retire to my hermit's cell by Thorney Pond and with my dog beside me ponder and plan my future very carefully. The varying seasons would mean visits to different parts of the country. I would even go so far as to estimate (as far as I can foresee the normal run of years) exactly how much time I had left to me, and would plan accordingly.

In January I should go North for some wild-fowling, returning perhaps at the end of the month. February, as a month, I dislike, and I would probably go abroad – I am not sure where – but April would call me back with memories of green lanes, pussy willows, and primroses in steep lane banks. I would remember a certain hostelry in Devon, down Chagford way, where I should spend the month trying to catch a salmon and possibly a trout in the Taw, and see the broken bright blue reflections of a spring sky through a palisade of alders.

The summer I would spend at home, for I could not miss my carp-fishing at Thorney; but as soon as the leaves of autumn fell I should go North again to my shooting- and fishing-box, either in Caithness or the Border country, which latter I know and love intimately, for it was there I caught my first salmon.

These visits would not be short; a fortnight would be the minimum.

Ah; the things we would do if we had the means! I have read of a man who won a vast fortune in some game of chance, whose sole ambition was to start a boarding-house in Blackpool or Clacton (I cannot remember which.... But I am wandering from the point.

If you are able and are content to follow your rod, it will take you to many a fair country and by many a fair stream.

One year I went to Waterville in County Kerry, staying at that comfortable hotel, the *Southern Lake*.

I loved Ireland, its green bogs and fuchsia hedges, its rough roads and shaggy mountains.

At times Waterville is excellent for trout, but in the year I was there the fishing was very poor. During my stay I never saw a single really heavy fish.

I caught nothing myself save a brace of one-pounders, and it seemed to me rather a dreary occupation rowing about the lake all day with only a few insignificant fish to show for one's trouble. I am never very happy in a small boat on deep water (the reason probably being that when a boy I was nearly drowned in the school swimming-bath).

One wild and blowy afternoon, my boatman (he was a boy of only sixteen or so) started to row across to an island in the middle of the lake. As we started away from the shelter of the bank, I could see white horses breaking out in the middle, and very soon we were among them with the water coming over the side into the boat.

The boy was too weak in the arm to manage the craft and soon became quite exhausted, bowed over his oars and white of face, while we drifted down the lake towards the sunken reefs at the far end, and all the time waves were breaking into the boat. It was an unpleasant experience.

There were several islands in the lake, one a desolate rocky place inhabited by wild goats, so my boatman told me.

I found the shooting much better than the fishing and I had some of the best duck- and snipe-shooting I have ever enjoyed, for luckily I had taken a gun with me.

One day, when we were out near the islands, a man in the next boat to ours, who was trout fishing, got into a salmon. All the morning, while we were drifting to and fro trying to make a catch of trout, I saw him with his rod bent in an arc, following the fish about. Eventually he was broken despite his gallant performance on such fine tackle.

There was one Blimpish old Colonel who spent every day drearily rowing right round the lake with a spinner over the stern, hoping for a salmon. He never had a single touch while I was staying at Waterville, and I suspect that he was more fond of boating than of salmon-fishing.

I did not try for salmon in the river, but other guests fished it, without result.

I may have given the impression that Waterville is no good for a fishing holiday, but this is not so. In some seasons wonderful catches are made both of salmon and trout; it just happened that I was there during a bad spell. Most fishing places have their ups and downs, including the delightful Border Esk where I fished for several seasons between the wars.

My favourite hostelry, the *Cross Keys* at Canonbie, seemed to me the ideal fisherman's inn, small and well-run, with excellent fare and a good cellar.

Moreover, the country is very lovely, fir-clad hills and oak woods reminiscent, in places, of the banks of the Wye, tumbling burns, and the high moors for those that like them.

As at Waterville, you may go to Canonbie and barely catch a sizeable fish, and again you may strike a lucky season and have the most wonderful sport. For the trout-fishing, May and the end of the season is the best, but I have had excellent herling in August from the two good pools above the Canonbie Bridge. Jock's Pool is sometimes a most entertaining water.

The *Cross Keys* is a good centre, for one is within reach of many tributary burns which flow into the Esk, and on occasion the Willow Pool below Canonbie is excellent for salmon.

I discovered this fishing inn by pure chance. I was motoring to Scotland one winter's day and had been delayed on the North Road by fog. I reached Carlisle after dark, and was tempted to stay at that place. It was lucky I decided to push on – luckier still that I ran into more fog between Carlisle and Langholm. As soon as I entered the door I knew that I was in the right type of fishing inn, not too pretentious, rods on the rack inside the door, thighboots and wading-trousers visible in odd corners, and a roaring fire in the lounge.

Heaven forfend I should ever stay at the so-called super fishing-hotel which bristles with waiters and cocktail bars. No good fishing inn serves an elaborate midday luncheon, but the breakfast is usually substantial and dinner the main meal. Such is (or was before the last war; and probably is still) the *Cross Keys*.

Every good fishing inn should have facilities for the instant drying of wet clothes, and plenty of hot water is essential. This latter is not always available in out-of-the-way inns. I like to be waited on by trim serving-maids in the good old black and white uniform, I like a touch of the bell to be answered promptly and with courtesy. I like to receive a welcome from the manager on my arrival, and for him to be in attendance at my departure.

Those who contemplate starting a fishing hotel please note these wants of the average angler!

I like to be able to enjoy a glass of a really good port after dinner, and to have a first-class Burgundy with it. I like to have for breakfast the trout that I catch, as an extra dish to the hotel breakfast, and the trout must be well cooked. Lastly I like to be awakened in the morning with a cup of tea presented to me by a damsel with a broad Scotch accent.

I admire the Scotch people enormously; the women are so neat and efficient, the men so unassuming and wiry. Your Scotch angler is a very canny fellow where trout are concerned, and I have yet to meet a jealous one.

In that land of misty hills, tumbling waters, purple moors, and the Lady Birch, the fisherman in his 'two-way' hat fits well into the landscpe. One senses a certain reverence for the big rivers of the North; even the smallest burn has a name, from its earliest beginnings. The Scotch do not speak of so-and-so living over the river, but 'across the Water' with a capital W.

In Langholm there is man who keeps a paper shop. His name is Adam Grieve. Many a time I have gone to Adam with my troubles. The water is low and stale, I have had no fish for a week. I go to him as an ailing man goes to his doctor.

'Well, Mr Grieve, I can't catch any fish. I suppose the river is hopeless now?'

'Aye, aye,' says Mr Grieve, 'It's low, but you can get the fish if you know how. I had seven herling last night up at Canonbie.'

If fish are to be caught, Adam Grieve will catch them. His skill is great, his knowledge passing wonderful.

He has the look of a true fisherman, a burly man with a merry red face, chubby and Pickwickian, just the sort of man to give much comfort to an angler whose 'patience is exhausted'. Adam's patience is never exhausted, and he has the great gift of putting a new edge to blunted enthusiasm.

When the water is low and stale he does most of his fishing by night with a white moth, a favourite fly on the Border Esk for night fishing.

What happy memories I have of night-fishing at Jock's Pool! The black firs on the far bank solemn and still, full of the melancholy hoots of owls, the loud chatter of the river as it sweeps round the bend into the still, rock-bound depths, the splash of a good fish jumping, invisible save for a faint gleam on the dark breast of the pool.

The thrill of night fishing on this river equals, I think, my midnight vigils at Thorney Pond, and the trout when hooked are equally difficult to bring to the net even though they are not half the weight of my Thorney carp.

One can only fish by 'feel'. With experience one can tell at once if one's fly is going out as it should, straight and true. And if you *do* get into one of those skipping herling, which, when they feel the prick of the hook describe a series of somersaults all down the pool, it takes all your skill before they are safely in the net. Many and many a one have I lost when I had him beaten and unseen on the shingle at my feet. Many a night I have gone up the rocky bank with an empty creel and heavy heart and seen the glow of a cigarette in the black shadows ahead. It would be Adam Grieve.

'Is that you, Mr Grieve?'
'Aye, aye.'
'Any luck?.'
'Aye, aye – four herling and a brown troot.'
I don't know how he does it....

Some years ago I caught my first salmon from the Esk – or rather, from the Black Esk, for above Langholm the river divides. It was late August and wild rainy weather had for some days made fishing out of the question; all the rivers were in spate. We filled in our time shooting over the wild hills of Eskdalemuir where I was staying with friends, in a charming house perched above the river. Fine woods surrounded us, and when we were not shooting or fishing they were delightful to wander in, and if one carried a gun there was often the chance of a pheasant. Being so high, Eskdalemuir gets a heavy rainfall, but some days the clouds blow away and the sun shines and I know no more lovely country when the weather behaves itself. There is a smell in the air which is quite indescribable: a keen peaty tang, the flavour of miles and miles of wild upland pastures and high moors. Sometimes I managed to collect a nice bag of mallard. The duck used to come up-river in the evenings. Once I stalked a party which had pitched behind some boulders in the river bed, and as they got up I downed three and had another with my second barrel.

There is something about those wild uplands which affects me powerfully, possibly because, on my mother's side, there is Border blood in my veins.

I suppose one's first salmon is as important a happening as the shooting of one's first goose, for until one has played and caught this King of Fish, one is not recognised as a complete angler.

About eight miles above Langholm Bridge the Esk divides, forming the White and Black Esk.

A pleasant road leads up through the Duke of Buccleuch's fir woods, a road which, when I knew it twenty years ago, was narrow and full of potholes. As soon as you climb above Langholm the woods are left behind and you can see the Esk on your right, winding serpent fashion through its beautiful valley, with here and there fine houses set among the woods upon its banks. Up and up you climb, past Harpsrig and Bentpath, where sheep lie upon the road and purple heather blooms. All the time, down on your right is the river, dark brown in its deeps, light ochre in the shallows, with shingle on the bends, bleached as white as bone.

Past Westerkirk, where Megget Water comes to swell the main river, on at last to Billholm Bridge which marks the junction of the two rivers, the White and Black Esk, and you come to 'Ticket Water'. Two hundred yards or so above Billholm Bridge the Black Esk takes a right-hand turn under a great hanging shaw. A massive ash tree grows on the north bank, and on the south side the river has striven with the naked rock and bored out a deep pool – a lovely salmon lie where I have twice had tussles with good fish and have twice been broken.

Spinning is not allowed for salmon on the Black Esk in August, otherwise I believe this would prove a deadly lure, for many pools are ideal for spinning.

When I fished the water I used a Jock Scott*, and it was on this that I hooked both salmon, both in the same week, though they were of course different fish.

The first one I lost through my own carelessness, a kink on the reel line; the second, a much heavier salmon, broke me round a rock.

I can imagine a keen fisherman getting out a map and looking at the very spot where I lost both these fish. I do the same thing myself when I am reading fishing-books wherein the author describes a certain river in detail.

It will be noticed that above the bridge the river has a little kink in it before it turns sharp left for Tanlawhill. This is the pool I am describing.

Did I think it likely that I should visit this pool once more, I would not give away such information; but I doubt very much if I ever again hear the merry rush of water at the throat of the pool, for my wanderings now take me otherwhere.

Should the reader ever find himself standing at that bend under the great ash, let him remember my words; and if he

---

* I have recently met a man who has done much salmon-fishing in the Border Esk, and he advises using a Peter Ross sea trout fly.

gets a salmon perhaps he will later lift a glass and drink to me a silent toast.

It was not in this pool, however, where I caught my first salmon.

If you fish this pool without result, follow the river up past Tanlawhill to where it takes a sudden turn to the left, forming almost a complete right-angle. If you have a map before you look well at this spot, because it is there that I caught my first salmon. That black thread-like line upon the page before you conveys nothing to you; you cannot picture the scenery as I saw it that August evening. I came to the river across a wide and rushy pasture, leaving my car in a disused quarry on the roadside above.

In front rose the bracken-covered hillside which leads up to Castle 'Oer and Allangillfoot. Bare and featureless, save for a fir wood near the crown, the great hillside mounts to the upper slopes and sky, roughened with bracken like the pile of a carpet. One can trace the road to Eskdalemuir by the slender black telegraph poles, but it is a long way up.

I wish I could remember the name of this pool, for, unlike the rivers of the Midlands, each pool has a name and therefore a personality.

It is long, deep, and very dark. On the field side there is a shingle ridge, which slopes steeply down into depths the colour of stout. Usually there are plates of buff foam spinning and wheeling under the far bank where, in August, red rowans glow against sombre bushes and overhanging trees.

That August evening, autumn seemed to be near. It always comes early to those wild hills. Low grey clouds drifted overhead from the west, and there was a considerable breeze which made casting difficult.

From time to time I heard the plaintive wailings of sheep, those faint lost cries which are ever audible in that lonely country, and there was a chill in the air which made me think that summer had gone for good.

I had had no luck lower down the river; the pool above Billholm Bridge had been drawn a blank, though I learnt from a shepherd that a fourteen-pounder had been caught there the evening before.

All that week there had been heavy rain and the river was just fining down; it seemed in perfect ply, just lightly coloured. I had not been fishing for more than five minutes before a great fish plunged near the tail of the pool. He

The fish made a circle of the pool and leapt once near
the tail, almost beaching himself on the shingle

came right out. Not long after, a smaller fish jumped, almost in the same place. I put the first fish at about fifteen pounds, the second in the region of seven or eight. One can estimate the weight fairly well if the fish jump clear.

Drawing a blank where the salmon had moved, I went up to the throat of the pool and fished it down twice without a sign. Perhaps, I thought, these were travelling fish, and were in no mood for taking, this blustery cold night.

At my second cast with the 'Palakona', on my third walk down, I was taken rather deep, about ten yards from the run in.

The fish made a circle of the pool and leapt once near the tail, almost beaching himself on the shingle.

Then he made a long run, evidently meaning to make a bid for the King Pool which is about a mile above. He did not get more than twenty yards round the bend when he thought better of it and came down again through the rough water into the deepest part of the pool – which was just what I wanted him to do.

He jumped twice more, and then it was a question of careful play. A quarter-of-an-hour later I saw his silver side gleaming in the peaty brown water, and I gaffed him (according to my diary) at six-fifteen, a cock salmon of fifteen pounds, with the sea lice on him. Probably the fish I saw jumping.

Gazing down at that gallant and splendid creature lying on the stones, I do not remember that I was aware of any great sense of triumph. I had killed my first salmon, but I was beyond the age when such a triumph gives rise to exultation; I did not feel half so pleased with life as when I landed my big trout from the Blythie. Perhaps I realised that now I had caught a salmon I had reached the heights of an angler's ambition, and that before me there were no higher peaks to which I might climb.

Looking back, the chief thing I seem to remember is the scarlet rowans tossing in the cold grey wind, the pale underside of their leaves gleaming against the dark bank opposite, and the far-away crying of sheep. Salmon must have travelled this road for a thousand years.

Above this pool, after a long scrambling stretch of water, is the King Pool. At first sight one would think that it should hold tremendous fish, but it is cold and cheerless with little shelter. The winds blow upon it through an opening in the rocks, and the waters come thundering down in a smother of foam.

Like woods, some pools are more lovable than others. The treeless King Pool is unlovable, and I always had a sense of great loneliness there, and desolation of spirit, even on sunny days.

Above the King Pool the Black Esk narrows rapidly and wanders away up among barren hills to the heights of Loch Fell, two thousand, two hundred and fifty feet above the sea.

There are, however, some excellent salmon lies, the best of which is not more than a hundred yards from the King Pool.

It is not really a pool at all but a deep steady run between rocks; still, it is a grand lie for salmon and far more profitable than the great King Pool itself.

I have never caught a salmon there, but I have been broken at least once, for jagged rocks lurk in the river bed.

I have had no experience in fishing the White Esk above Eskdalemuir, but there is good trouting up to the bridge and a few salmon-pools which, however, never seem to hold big fish. Much of it is 'Ticket Water'. In any case, the Esk is not a river where one may expect heavy salmon. I believe I am right in saying that the record is not above thirty pounds.

There are other good rivers in this lovely country, and I once spent a most enjoyable holiday at Newcastleton, an ugly little town which lies to the east of Langholm. The stretch from Newcastleton to Kershopefoot is an excellent sea-trout water and holds some good brown trout too. This river, the Liddel, joins the Esk above Longtown and I have had more fish from it than from the Esk. I know nothing of this water between Newcastleton and Liddelbank, save the upper reaches below and above the town. It is much less expensive than the Esk. As far as I remember, the Canonbie ticket was three pounds odd for the week, and this did not include salmon. You can (or could) fish the Liddel at Newcastleton for a few shillings a week, but I doubt if it would be worth a visit unless the water was in good ply, for it is, for the most part, a shallow, stony river.

CHAPTER XII

THE UNTOUCHABLE

Would you (I wonder) care to come with me up the Byremill Burn? What chance is there of sport with this low water, you ask? None at all in the Esk, I should say, unless you are of the calibre of Adam Grieve, which, forgive my saying so, you are not. You may challenge anyone on your own ground, the chalk streams of the South; but this type of river fishing in hot weather has beaten you. I intend to go out this evening, however, clear-water worming, which, of course, is a closed book to you....

Now, my dear fellow, I may be an Untouchable in this matter of the worm, but believe me, the art is not so easy. Listen to reason. Here you are, after six days' fishing, the water low and stale, and every day unclouded sun. You have not had a fish. Of course not: they are all so sick and stale themselves, they have no appetite. The salmon are lying in the pools, fed to their gibs, and all the sea trout have no doubt gone back to the sea in disgust. No, I must correct that statement.

Only yesterday forenoon, at the tail of Jock's Pool, I was sitting on a big rock, contemplating those 'various little

Here we are at the little stone bridge where the dipper builds each spring, right under the arch among the ivy

living creatures that are fed by the God of Nature', as old Walton quaintly puts it; and I noticed that the base of this rock was submerged in a stale brown pool some two feet deep. Between this pool and the main river was a thin film of water which covered a shingle bank.

I investigated this almost landlocked pool, where the small pebbles on the bottom were green with slime, and thought I detected a movement right under the rock, where there was a deep cranny. I picked up a piece of 'spate' wood and poked it under. Out shot a magnificent sea trout of quite eight pounds; it was certainly the best sea trout I have ever seen in the Esk.

It dashed around the pool and went straight at the shingle bank, flapped desperately for a moment, and slipped away into the main river.

This trout must have been imprisoned here since the last spate. Such happenings are frequent at this time of year and have been noted by others.

But to return to your lack of success. It is not good for a man like you to go fishless for so many days. I have been observing you covertly of late, sitting gloomily in the lounge at nights, fiddling with your fly box. You are as stale as the river; a few nice trout in the basket would work wonders. What! You will never fish with the worm? Then you shall act as my ghillie, just for one evening, and I promise you we shall get a fish or two. You will? Sensible fellow!

Here we are at the little stone bridge where a dipper builds each spring, right under the arch among the ivy. If it were not for the barbed-wire and those new plus-fours you are wearing, I would show you the old nest.

Notice how the rowans hang over the burn, just by the sheep-boom on which wreckage of last year's floods still adhere. You think no trout worthy of my basket lives in such a puny burn? I hope soon to disillusion you.

We will fish up the left bank. I know this burn well. I have a great affection for it. Perhaps it was this burn which first disclosed to me the delights of the hermit's life, for after the first war, my lungs rotten with gas, I came here with a tent. Soon I will show you where I lived for three weeks with only the burn, trout, and dippers to comfort me. I will show you the exact spot where I pitched my habitation, on a level little mead among the oaks, almost completely encircled by the scrambling burn. Its cold clear waters served as wine, and a very lovely wine it was; and when I felt so inclined, I climbed the purple hill up there and shot a grouse or rabbit for the pot, all through the kindness of the Admiral, God give him in peace. At night I lay in my blanket-bag and listened to the voice of the Byremill, and so life was good after all.

Here, as we go up under the scrub oaks and alders, there are no good fish, only little barred 'smouts', though the latter make a wonderfully good fry for a hungry man. Do not look so pained – Nature provides enough salmon parr to offset such depredations.

You will notice how, wherever there are streams, the alder grows. It is the same all over our land. North or South; the alder is *the* tree which cannot thrive far from water.

You will notice that these trees are closing in as the glen becomes more narrow. Each Border glen is to pattern, well-grown trees, oaks, ashes, and alders, near where they meet the main river; firs perhaps and larches; higher up, more firs, sometimes crowding thick and dark about the burn, overarching it. We shall come to such a wood higher up. Then, as we climb higher, more stunted oaks and finally rowans, and the open moor. Follow still higher and there is no growth at all, simply the bleached bents, heather, bleating diminutive hill-sheep and shaggy hares.

On the far side of the wall you may notice the harvest, late, as always, in this part of the world. Though this is early September, the corn is still in stook. Those large black birds which you possibly imagine are crows or black fowls (your knowledge of ornithology leaves much to be desired, and you suffer from not being a shooting-man), those large black birds, I say, are blackcock, and a very handsome bird is the male with his lyre-shaped tail – the red grouse never descend this far. Maybe higher up we shall surprise a few of them by the burn, feeding on the rowan berries. They perch on walls and trees as happily as wood pigeons, a thing I have never seen a red grouse do. The latter will frequently perch on boulders in the heather and *occasionally* on walls, but for the most part they keep to the very highest tops of these hills.

Look at the evening sun shining on that purple hill crown. I can hear a curlew up there though I cannot see it; it is just a Voice among the heather, a sort of familiar spirit of the Border country. How much better this, than brooding over your sorrows and well-thumbed fly box in the lounge!

Now the burn takes a bend. There is a pool there under the alder, not deep or long, but a good hold for a brown trout. I do not think that even you will look askance at this gossamer cast with its single shot a foot above the hook. Here is a wriggling red worm, dug this morning by the old man at the inn – Jamie is a fisherman himself, and once he asked me to go salmon-poaching with him, a great compliment. And did I? In the circumstances, and remembering in whose company I am, I think I will not say....

Now I take the red wriggler from its bed of moss – you need not look, if you have not a manly stomach.... There – he is threaded through the head. Stand here and imagine that I am stalking one of your Test trout. You will see me crawl to the bank of the burn and throw a long line, not an easy matter with these over-arching alder boughs. But my little Hardy 'Itchen' 9½-footer is a wizard in confined quarters. There – the worm has landed well up the pool, right in the very scurry of the neck of it. The current bears it swiftly at first; I am well below, crouched among the ferns; no fish can see me.

As the current slows and is spent, the worm swings in a little towards the bank... There – what did I tell you! – a nice brown trout. Now do your stuff with the net, for on this fine tackle it is no child's play. This is a very different matter, let me tell you, from fishing the spate. Then the shepherd boys catch trout on a clothes-line and an eel-hook; even I have too much self respect to use a worm then.

Gently now, here he comes, close on half-a-pound if he's an ounce. Well done! We have him, rather big-headed perhaps, but spotted and tricked out most handsomely. Three more like him and I shall have a breakfast.

Here is the place where my tent was pitched. The blackened circle of my long dead fire is not to be seen, but someone else has been camping here, a little higher up. A tinkler no doubt. It is amazing how these tinklers (not tinkers please) infest Scotland. The higher you go, and the wilder the country, the more you will find. It amazes me how the English 'gippos' live, but how the tinkler keeps body and soul together I just do not know. At Braemar, when the Gathering is on, they sell white heather; the

Gathering is to the Scottish tinkler what the Derby is to our Romany Rye.

When I camped here, years ago, there was a shepherd who sometimes favoured me with a visit and partook of the comfort of my fire; a sturdy, good man, whose whole life had been spent upon these wild hills. He spoke such broad Scotch I could hardly follow him, but we had many a crack beside my fire and he told me many things which he had seen, many of which were passing strange.

He described how he has often snared a salmon, higher up, in the breeding season, and he has watched their mating. That is a sight I have never seen, but I would commend to your notice a book by that grand old sportsman, Abel Chapman, wherein he describes the mating of the King of Fishes in his own Northumberland burns.

Here we are at the sheep-gate. Beyond is the dark fir wood. We will enter in and follow up the burn.... I see you are having difficulty: a strand of wire has laid hold upon your jacket button. Allow me...

Have you ever considered what useless things are buttons? Have you ever counted the number of buttons an average man carries about with him through life? They are like salmon lice. You are counting now I see.... Over twenty? – I thought so! Some men even wear buttons on top of their caps, and (not so long ago) upon their boots.

Now the sound of the water is loud and echoing, the gloom is deep, it is as if we were in a scented tunnel. The only light comes from the opening higher up, and this light shines upon the flat faces of the pools and crinkled runs.

Strange to say, I have caught a good trout here in this shadowed wood. I will stalk that pool yonder above the rock – the rock itself will afford good cover. The line has twitched, though I cannot see over the rock. I strike and – yes! I have another, a mere banded 'smout'.

Sometimes when I have been fishing this gloomy place alone I have been smitten with a sudden unreasoning fear. I have imagined that voices are calling to me above the music of the waters, or strange bells chiming.

Here we are at the end of the fir wood. It will be pleasant to feel the wind on our faces, and the sun.

But first let me try that pool on the bend, just before we come to the sheep-boom. It is a well-loved haunt of a good trout. How strange it is that trout have a liking for one particular lie; in the midlands and the south this is especially so. I dare swear that, could I but return to the self-same pool where I caught my big trout below Tansy Mill, there would be another awaiting me.

That was a good cast. The worm, a fresh one just put on, landed up in the swift water just as I wanted it to do. I can feel the gentle 'scurr' of the single shot knocking on the stones as the bait is hurried down towards us. The fish (if fish is there) will have his back to us, for he will be facing upstream.

I have him – by the Venerable Izaak, I have him, and it is no brown trout but a herling; and a good herling at that, worthy of Adam Grieve himself.

Steady – now he's taking me up the burn. See, he leaps once, twice, thrice – two pounds if he's an ounce! A murrain on him! Plague take him! He's off! That corkscrew skip, how I abominate it! Never mind, his skill is the greater. It was no fault of mine that I lost him. Perhaps if you had been.... But that is idle talk. There is another pool, a still brown pool I wot of, above the alders there, close to that round stone sheep-pen.

Now look around you. You had not realised that we have climbed so high or so far. You cannot see the Esk; it is hidden by the Douglas firs by the Admiral's house. Over there you can see Tinnis Hill above Langholm, Hartsgarth Hill, and many more, silvery pale in the evening sun.

One day I will bring you to Langholm for the Common Riding, and you shall see the Cornet mounted on his horse, the most envied and sought-after young yeoman in all the Border Lands on that great day.

But we are at the pool. It lies at the bend under ubiquitous alders; above it the green wall of bracken rises, dotted with graceful silver birch. Fat maggots of sheep move across the side of the shadowed hill which towers above, all in line. As they come to a burnlet they jump, one after the other, flop, flop, like woolly mops.

My first cast is a bad one and becomes hitched on the alders. A gentle pull with the hand frees it. It falls with a plop into the pool and is taken at once by a good trout. We must have him out as quietly and as swiftly as we may, for there will be other fish here – the pool is a long one. That makes two for the basket.

Three good brown 'troots' I draw from this pool, all of a size, three-quarters-of-a-pound apiece. Then I miss one and it is time to go.

The setting sun still glows upon the Admiral's hill top. High-flying gulls slowly pass, bound for the Solway. The shadows from the grouse butts stretch long on the heather and, yes, there is the 'back, go back' of a red grouse. Had you been a shooting-man that sound would stir you as the cry of geese does me, or the clamour of hounds by a winter cover rouses the hunting-man. These sounds stir us because we associate them with the chase. Some people cannot understand this hunting instinct; they say all sport is 'cruel'. But their ideas are wrong-headed. When I tell you that only this year I saw a fox leave cover with hounds on his brush and – lo! – running in the middle of the pack, also after the fox, was another fox! Surely that gives food for thought? I have seen a fox toiling after the pack which had 'gone away' after his brother. He seemed puzzled and disappointed when they left him behind.

I have caught fish with one of my former hooks in his mouth, a trout which I had played and lost only a few minutes before. There is the classic story of the perch which was caught with its own eye; a rather horrid story, but true nevertheless.

Draw this pure wind down into your lungs; it is the finest in Britain, I do believe. A champagne among all airs, a wine of the finest vintage.

Already, friend, if I may say so, you look better; the eye is brighter, you self-respect restored. You are glad you came? Of course you are. But see! – the sun is off the hill. Soon the owls will be calling in the fir woods, and we have to go back through the haunted glen. As we are together it does not matter perhaps: the kelpies (for kelpies surely dwell there) will not disturb two mortals in company; it is the single men they will assail.

And also (I must confess it without shame) I have an appetite. Now I come to think of it, it is a very *insistent* appetite. I had been so engrossed with my fishing (and your company) that this subtle, oft-repeated demand from my lower anatomy was overlooked. Now thoughts turn to a bath; of tables set with starched napery; the piquant nose and green eyes of Jeanie as she hands the soup. And, let me whisper it, my spies tell me that there is sea trout for the fish course and partridge to follow.

CHAPTER XIII

SHADOWS AND REFLECTIONS

I dislike the art of fishing to be termed a hobby or a pastime; to me it amounts to much, much more. A 'hobby' suggests some dreadful fretwork business, and 'pastime' has an evil ring about it. I have never wanted to 'pass' the time; its rate of progress is already exceeding the speed limit. There is, somewhere ahead of us all, a certain fixed point where time will pass *us* with a thoroughness and unconcern which is, in a world of shifting sands, the one predictable happening. The hard and fast rules, the regulations of Nature, are immensely comforting to me, the one undeniable fixed fact in my awareness. I must obey these laws or perish; there are no half measures. Such all-powerful stern Authority is good for man's feeble soul.

The only thing which causes me sorrow is that, like the mayfly, our sojourn by Life's river is so short. I find myself sometimes envying the alders who have been granted a longer stay and whose roots will be refreshed by the sweet waters long after I have gone hence.

I notice you are almost asleep; in fact I think I detected a diminutive snore. The good dinner you have provided and your own excellent port are proving too much for you, and my bumbling discourse has put the seal upon your eyelids.

Talking of mayflies, I saw quite a number this morning. I should have some sport tomorrow if this weather holds. A more appropriate name would be June fly, because I have rarely seen a big hatch in May. Nor does May invariably bloom in May with the wonder it displays in June.... But I perceive your head has now sunk upon your breast; your lips twitch, your right hand fingers also, as they lie upon your knee. Perhaps you are playing some fantastic dream trout, as my dog pursues his dream rabbits.

By the yelps and growls my dog makes when he is so employed, I think he gets a deal of fun out of his dream hunting; but when all is said and done, it is a poor shadowy substitute for the real thing.

Yes, it was a perfect day. That old Cotswold house where I was staying deserves description as I saw it on that superb morning in early June.

If you, the reader, know of any other more delectable country than this valley of the Colne in Gloucestershire, then I would bid you direct me thither. But first be silent and hearken to my story:

The time is a little after seven in the morning and the world without so marvellous that it is a crime to be within even these graceful walls. Through the mullioned window I see the shaven green lawn sloping to the river not a bow-shot away, sparkling and winking in the bright light. Have you ever seen such a lovely stream and such noble trees? I know no other trees which reach such fulfilment of grace, stature, and beauty as these in the valley of the Colne. In the copper beech, whose new leaves I can see from my bed, a blackbird has been warbling since dawn (one would have thought his throat was weary with so much carolling), and from all about other birds are praising God: they at any rate have the grace to be thankful.

On the lawn, which is still moist with the early dews, a fox-hound pup is playing a game of make-believe all by himself, as a child plays. He chases his tail, he races away round the bole of the copper beech, comes back to the lawn centre, and flops down for a moment, looking at the house, his ears now alive for noises from the kitchen. But how can he remain still for a moment? In an instant he is seized with a frenzy, he rushes like a mad thing around and about, uttering little suppressed yelps of ecstasy. He too praises the 'God of Nature' for this gift of life on a June morning.

Now and again through the wide-open window comes the murmur of the waterfall at the end of the lawn where the Colne has been arrested in its course by an artificial dam.

A furling ring appears and dies on the sliding breast of the stream. Some truly weighty trout dwell in this pool, but they are not to be angled for: they are the spoilt darlings of my hostess. My host would fain catch them, and this (let me whisper) he has been known to do on oocasion when the Lady of the Manor is elsewhere. You cannot suppress the hunting-instinct entirely.

No small wonder that he despises my pitiful litle pond at home, my mean hut and solitary vigils! Did I live here, perhaps I should be equally scornful.

Above this dam near the limit of the ground there is another pool where only yesterday eve I saw many large and aldermanic trout rising. There are chestnuts there, overhanging the water, and now these magnificent trees are arrayed in their full glory.

There my host threw pieces of bread upon the waters. We watched them drift under the chestnut candles and, with many a gulp and boil, each fugitive crust was drawn below. I am not trusted there when evening falls; there is no knowing what an Untouchable might be up to.

This house seems to have grown like a tree upon this lovely river's brim; it has grown as naturally and as beautifully as those gracious pillars of foliage. In those days, when men built a house, they were much closer to Nature, they could not build an ugly thing. Even the barns, the cottages, the farm houses, show this, each in its way so perfect, so in harmony with its surroundings.

Notice with what care the roofs are tiled, how the upper tiles are very small, becoming larger as they descend to the roof-edge. This gives an illusion of height, it makes for dignity. We do not trouble about such trivialities today. Blue slates, all of a size, are what I see in the Midlands, where most permanent houses are as ugly as the dreadful 'Prefabs'.

But my nose suggests breakfast. There is a faint aroma of coffee in the room which was not noticeable a moment ago. This first smell is the trumpeter of others; bacon I soon

There are chestnuts there, overhanging the water, and now these magnificent trees are arrayed in their full glory.

identify and, if I mistake not, trout.

Every homely house should give forth such smells at the appointed hour.

The fox-hound pup on the lawn, whose nose is keener than mine and more sensitive to such matters, has already vacated the dew-dabbled lawn, and nothing but the little dark marks of his pads show that he has been there. The blackbirds and thrushes have also ceased to sing so loudly; they too have gone in search of their second breakfast.

It is time to descend and see what lies under the silver covers on the sideboard, which I will investigate as a hungry bullhead rolls a stone on a stream bed; and after that I will look to my lines and tackle, for the fishes' appetites will also need assuaging on such a morning. I shall be only too happy to wait upon them.

I cross the mown lawn, climb an iron railing where wild rose buds cluster, and walk across a single meadow under tall lime trees to the river. These limes have thick twiggy growths half-way up their stems; a species of parasite, I believe, and one to which the lime is particularly subject. As I pass under, a stock dove shoots out with a clatter. They like building right in among the tangled thicket. In early July you may smell these limes for many meadows distant, the last fragrant smell of summer and one which I associate with tench-taking and carp-catching.

Before the trees hide the house, I look back to enjoy the aspect of its mellow tiles and gables, and am dismayed, nay annoyed, to see that the fox-hound pup has followed. In the ways dogs will when they are not wanted, he stands with a tentative wag of his tail, looking intently at my eyes to study my reactions. If I smile now at his earnest face, or speak a commiserating word, he will be upon me in an instant, and fishing will be out of the question for the rest of the day. So I assume an air of strong disapproval, I point towards the house like a stern headmaster reproving a boy caught out of bounds, and the pup turns about with in-tucked tail and lopes back sulkily to the iron fence, turning once again, however, to see if by chance I have relented. It is very hard to have to tell him that he cannot come, and I feel inhuman, a spoil-sport. I like a dog's desire to share good things with his lord and master; it is pathetically touching. A dog will always prefer to walk with a man in preference to another of his own kind, save when he is seeking a mate.

The cuckoos are calling over the valley, the mass of trees are yet pearly with the morning, the grass studded with flowers, buttercups and cuckoo pints; lately-arrived swifts hurry in dusky bands high overhead, screeching thinly as they race.

The stream is reached. Compared with a Scotch river such as the Esk, this seems almost an ornamental plaything, it is so gentle and exquisite. Six or seven strides and you would be across it; nor would it come higher than your waist. I could sit here on such a morning, hour after hour, watching this aquarium of nature which is as clear as glass. The dense beds of graceful waving water-weed add to its attraction, those stirring thickets which sway and wag with the current. I begin to see why I am regarded as an Untouchable. My opaque deeps of Thorny Pond — how can you compare them?

There are disappointingly few mayfly, though it is the second of June. The main hatch has yet to come. The reason is that this spring has been perverse and sulky. We have had no settled spell of warmth until two days ago.

Small broken fragments of weed come hurrying by — someone must be weed-cutting up above Bibury. They travel so smoothly on the breast of the clear stream, and in a moment they are gone. It will not be long before they join the Thames at Lechlade, in an hour or so maybe, and a delightful voyage too on such a morning.

Only an odd mayfly is seen dancing over the grass, but the Olive Duns are plentiful and this decides me to put one on. Yet still I am loathe to fish. Thank goodness the keeper is not with me, waiting impatiently for me to start!

A yard or so away, in the tail of big cress-beds, lies a trout. It is a fish of about a pound, finely spotted. He sways in the current as if tethered by his nose, and the tail is constantly sweeping and fluttering. He remains in the same spot, and now and again I see the whitish underpart of his mouth as he gives an extra puff. He is like a kestrel hovering in a stream of air, he has all the time to be adjusting his trim and balance against the push of the flow. I watch him for ten minutes, and he never once shows any interest in passing Olives! and in any case I do not want to disturb him. He fascinates me.

Is there anything better than a trout lying thus in a crystal stream? How strange it is that we wish to twitch it forth and expose that cold, wonderfully-wrought creature to the upper airs! I grant you that he would be very nice to eat but what belly-pleasure can compare with the spirit-pleasure of watching such a perfect fish in such a perfect stream?

I do not get this feeling with my Thorney carp, which, even in their more robust way, are very beautiful. The trout is such a *well-bred* fish (as is the salmon), and I suppose that is why refined people prefer to angle for them.

To the coarse mind a trout is no different from a herring. Many of us have seen salmon caught in nets as though they were cod, a most shocking sight to a sensitive man with any refinement in him.

It is this feeling of respect which made R. W. lay aside his gaff when he had the record carp at his mercy – and a very proper feeling too, for the carp is a gentleman. I would not hestitate a moment to gaff a pike or a barbel. It always pains me to gaff a salmon. The rule of landing salmon with a net on the Shiel, for instance, is most correct. The salmon is too lovely a creature to stab with steel; his silver side should not be marred by blood.

But I must have a fish to show to my host when he returns, and so I must be up and doing. When I rise gently to my feet among the flowery grasses, the trout I have been admiring for so long has gone, though I never saw his departure. A cuckoo flies swiftly by with his spotty Chinese plumage, and a hysterical swarm of swallows crowd about his tail. With a defiant 'Cuck-cuck-cuckoo!' he vanishes into a mound of white hawthorn round which the swallows dither and depart. Trout are moving farther down. Now and again I see a dimple on the glassy smoothness. My Olive Dun floats onwards and at the limit of the cast a trout takes it and dives straight into a forest of wagging weed, burrowing into it like a rabbit in a woodpile, to regret his mistake at leisure.

Hand-lining soon tells, and after a fight which lasts, I suppose, five minutes, he is ready for the net, a trim fish of a pound-and-a-half.

I will not weary the reader with the account of the other five fish I caught, or the six I returned, or the one (the biggest of course – actually he was probably a two-pounder, but he pulled like a four-pounder) which weeded me so effectively, by the bridge, that my fine cast parted.

The salmon is too lovely a creature to stab with steel;
his silver side should not be marred by blood

I do not know what the record trout is for the Colne, but I have an idea that it is in the region of six-pounds – though not from this beat.

I could have caught more, but it was the morning that entranced me, the indescribable loveliness of it. I have never had the good fortune to fish the Test or Itchen, though I have seen those waters in high June and know that they are lovely too. But for perfect beauty give me this wooded valley with its massive trees and restful houses, the golden seas of buttercups, the snow-laden hawthorns.

I did not return for luncheon as I had intended (who could think of food on such a day?). At noon I lay down in the meadow, in the shade of a hawthorn, and opened my basket to look at my catch, laid tastefully on its bed of reeds. Only the coarse-minded angler stuffs his fish into his basket without giving them a soft green shroud. They seemed alive, those spotted beauties, thick of body, small of head. But already their minted freshness was departing, the tails stiff. Looking at them I felt a pang of sorrow which I had never experienced before. Perhaps it was the thought that I had taken their lives on such a lovely day: they were too beautiful to die. And as I lay among the cool green grass with the perfume of hawthorn about me, looking at these fish, another inquiring, peering face was thrust over my shoulder, and I received a warm wet slap of a tongue and a puff of doggy breath. It was the fox-hound pup. It had followed me, had stolen upon me as I lay beneath my flowery-scented tent.

Instead of being angry (I dislike disobedience in dogs as I do in children), I forgave him and pulled his soft ears, and was glad to watch him and have him near me. It mattered not to him, perhaps, that this was so perfect a day, that he could not sense or see the magic of June.

I told him that soon these days, these happy carefree days of puppy-hood, must end, and that soon he would (if he proved to be a well-grown hound) find other pleasures and stern masters, and must learn obedience and good manners; that his true life was not to be spent in aimlessly wandering about a lovely garden, or lying in the sun, or chasing his tail.

One day he would chase another sort of tail, a red bushy brush, attached to the hinder end of a sly little red gentleman who would lead him many a dance in a cold winter world of woods, sodden upland pastures, and wet stone walls.

His gods then would be other gods, in pink coats mounted on fine horses – not a tweedy, idle man lying under a hawthorn bush on a summer's day. And, my homily over, I shut the lid of my basket, picked up my rod, and together we went slowly back over those meadows of Paradise to a mellow old house where long shadows were already stealing to meet the stream and a gracious lady was preparing a dish of tea upon the lawn.

CHAPTER XIV

A MIXED BAG

There is one type of angling which even I, a confirmed coarse-fisher, cannot enjoy, and that is canal fishing.

I think that he who fishes canals in preference to other waters has the match-fisher's mind, and he would not be happy unless others were lined up alongside, with plenty of beer and questionable stories in circulation.

I know very well that in some districts, industrial centres, the canal is probably the only possible ditch where a man may put in a line (for when all is said and done, a canal *is* but a ditch and nothing more, a mere trench full of dirty water). I suppose it is better to angle in a canal than not to angle at all, and I shall be regarded as a pampered and spoilt person who can, if he so wishes, go north, south, east, or west in quest of sport and have access to good waters. I fear that this is true.

I always remember some years ago giving a man permission to fish in Thorney Pond for roach. He came, if I recollect aright, from the Warrington district, and was a hard-working fellow who had a real passion for fishing. He caught about twenty medium roach. He was overjoyed. He told me that he never caught such fish in his own waters, and seemed beside himself with delight.

I thought then what a good thing it would be if poor hard-working fellows in industrial areas could be helped to stock good waters, how wealthy Corporations could, if they wished, either make, provide, or rent, fishing-lakes, where the angling section of the poorer folk could enjoy themselves. I feel I have said hard things about fishing-matches and fishing-clubs, and it may be that I have been churlish in this respect. Any man who fishes is a friend of mine and one of the Brotherhood. I cannot help feeling, however, that if circumstance had so ordained that I should be forced to live in a grimy industrial area, I should, in my free time, go off by myself and seek other waters where I could be alone, even if it entailed a long cycle journey. If this were not possible, then I don't think (you will notice that I am not sure), I don't think that I would fish at all.

But to return to canals. Fond as I am of water, I cannot whip up my enthusiasm over this artificial highway. Nature does her best with it, adorning the banks in places with wild roses and reeds; even water-lilies strive to appear after a generation. But its utilitarian aspect can never be disguised. It has not the happy carefree meanderings of a stream or river which takes its leisurely course, that of least resistance, through flowery meadows. The fish that swim in canals are mostly undersized, quite inedible; and for some reason or another they tend to ignore the angler's lures.

Some years ago I fished a glorified canal, one of the Fenland levels, for bream. Arthur Ransome has, I believe, likened these levels to flooded railway cuttings, and no better simile do I know. Unlike the inland waterways, they hold big fish. I caught a very large bream of five pounds or so on my first evening, but the week I spent there was miserable. I hated the straight highway of water stretching to the horizon, the level, treeless banks. This, I think, shows the difference between the Izaak Walton type of angler and he who is simply out to catch fish, he of the 'fishmonger' mind.

To enjoy our sport as it should be enjoyed, our surroundings must be beautiful, for your true angler enjoys nature as much as he enjoys fishing.

The only types of canal that have ever attracted me are those disused canals and arms, old ruined lock-basins and so forth, where no traffic has passed for years. There the water is no longer the yellow-ochre, opaque liquid which is so familiar. It is clear and bright, water weeds abound, trees and bushes flourish, birds frequent the banks, and the fish are often larger and bolder biters than those in used canals.

A word must be said about moats. Here there is definitely an attraction, even though they are usually narrow and canal-like. All moats are ancient. This gives them an immense advantage. There is no traffic to disturb the water and churn up the mud. They are usually adjuncts to a romantic and lovely dwelling, whether manor or castle; water-lilies flourish, and carp grow to noble proportions. And I would remind you that moats are rarely rectangular.

I frequently think that I should like to live in a moated manor house, especially if the moat contained carp. It would not be long before I invented some sort of night-fishing contrivance with an alarm-bell. I think it would be amusing to lie in bed, snug and warm, and think of big fish approaching my bait in the deep cold waters below my bedroom wall. The playing of a big carp, if one were clad only in pyjamas, on a dark night, with plenty of lily beds in the vicinity, has exciting possibilities; but it would be a sport only to be enjoyed by bachelors who have not quite grown up; fancy toys with the notion of long-handled landing nets, of powerful searchlights which might be switched on when the fish was hooked. But what one would do once the fish were 'landed', I have not yet made up my mind. A big carp in one's bedroom might be embarrassing. Of course, one could always drop it back again, but that would not be fishing.

To be serious, however. There is no reason why, if one is so unfortunate as to possess a moat, one should not have first-rate angling on one's doorstep, especially if the mud were dredged from time to time. And there would be a real fascination for me in hearing the big carp leaping, as they do on summer nights, in the solemn deeps below my walls.

The charm of river fishing is obvious. For the rather restless type of angler there is the opportunity for travel, leisurely travel with new vistas and new scenes at every bend and turning (I have spent many delightful summer days rambling along the banks of the Ouse); or if you feel in contemplative mood, you can settle down and fish some deep quiet reach as if it were a pond. This is where a big river has the advantage over a landlocked pond; it can cater for so many tastes and moods. Moreover, big rivers hold big fish, and this again is an incentive.

The rivers of the Midlands, though at first sight appearing tame to the Northener, are, in reality, more attractive to the fisherman-naturalist. A Scottish river has rarely any luxuriant bank growth; in summer there is invariably a band of dry shingle scattered with rocks. The leisurely winding 'coarse fish' river is never without some interest; its level hardly ever varies – at least, not to the extent of the swift rocky water – and one is lured along its banks with greater insistence. The weir; the mill, with its willows and its ponderous wooden wheel; the luxuriant riverside growth, so diverse and beautiful, its many water-loving birds – these attractions are not found in the mountain-born water. There is a great pleasure to be had in the heats of June and July, stalking the great lazy chub as they lie beneath the shadow of the willows and hawthorns. They are quite as shy as trout. I have no love for the chub, however. It is a handsome creature, boldly scaled, red of fin and pleasantly coloured; but it is inedible unless cooked by an expert, and after the first two minutes of fight it loses heart and allows itself to be towed in like a sodden log.

I have caught big chub in the Severn out of runs which are likely holds for salmon. I have caught them when trout-fishing in the Border Esk; for, strange to say, they are all too common in some parts of that river above Canonbie. On hot days you can see them lying near the surface of the pools close inshore, and at first sight the heart leaps as one mistakes them for big trout. But a second look fills one with disgust: there is something highly improper about chub frequenting a salmon and trout water.

If one prefers movement, both of water and the legs and arms God gave one, I should prefer the chalk streams. There you have all the good points of the mountain stream and the sluggish river combined. You have the fascination of clear, swiftly-running water and sporting fish, and also the attraction of wild flowers and riverside life.

I shall never forget some years ago, when fishing a chalk stream with the dry fly, coming upon some men weed-cutting. They were wading up the centre of the stream, plying their scythes as though they were mowing a meadow. So hard and clean was the stream bed that the water below them was hardly clouded, only particles of floating weed came down the current to be raked out by a man who was waiting two hundred yards below the reapers. He was also up to his middle in the stream.

Beside him, among the fresh grass and crushed flowers, was a mound of the wet weed, quite unattractive in itself now that it was out of its element. Water-mints and crowfoot, when they are swayed in a crystal clear current, are alluring, but when the plants are cut and raked-out they are as unattractive as a heap of my Thorney Pond weed.

What tickled my fancy, however, on that hot June day was the fact that in the adjacent meadow the hay crop was also being cut. The men in the field were sweating and hot, whereas the men in the stream appeared cool and to be enjoying themselves.

These chalk streams are usually very cold, far more chill than a Midland river. I have swum on a boiling day in a chalk stream, but have never been able to stay in for any length of time.

When chub fishing on the Ouse in hot summer weather, I have frequently stopped at intervals during the day and for twenty minutes or so have pretended to be a water-vole. It is delicious to thread the beds of reeds and willow-girt bays, to skirt the lily beds and sunken trees, to let the slow current bear one along over deep and shallow. This one can never do in a Northern stream or river. I sometimes swim at night in Thorney Pond, and an uncanny sensation it is. After a hot day the upper layer of water is pleasantly warm and stays so until the early hours, but it is unwise to drop the legs. Three feet from the surface it is deadly cold, and those that suffer from cramp are asking for trouble if they swim alone at night.

I have never been an expert swimmer: I know no fancy strokes; I dislike 'crawls' and 'dog paddles'. A slow breast stroke is my favourite, and I like to make as little noise as possible. I often think it is a pity that the human body, ill-adapted as it is for swimming, cannot glide silently through the water as a fish does. The nearest one can come to this motion is by swimming on the back; but even then the arms have to be working all the time, and though the sweeps may be leisurely, one cannot stop all motion and glide like a fish.

The only possible way I have found is to use 'water-wings' – or even an old motor tyre – but this is not true swimming.

The speed with which a fish can move through the water is amazing: even though he is streamlined, it is difficult to see how a carp, for instance, can shoot along under the surface at such high speed. But if one examines the build of a carp one notices at once the powerful shoulders and the large muscular fins which are spoon-like. The tench has even more powerful pectoral fins, and they are even more spoon-shaped, but I have never found them move with the swiftness of a hooked carp; they have not the streamlined body. If the carp attaines its high rate of motion by its big pectoral fins, the salmon does so by its tail, which is broad and massive. The tail of the carp is, of course, fairly strong, but it has not the square end of the salmon's tail; it is slightly forked.

In addition to his powerful front fins, the carp has a long dorsal, which I believe also acts as an additional screw. No other coarse fish has such a lengthy dorsal fin; it reaches almost to the tail.

I believe the barbel is a fast mover when hooked, but I have had no experience of these shark-faced fish, which I believe are quite inedible and which some maintain are actually poisonous on the table. They are the oddest-looking creatures, almost eel-like in their slim length. Yet they are beautiful, close-scaled and with graceful lines, the only ugly feature being the head with its small sulky mouth overhung by a sinister nose which gives them a Jewish appearance. One day I must try my hand at barbel-fishing, as they run large, well over the ten-pound mark, are magnificent fighters, and therefore worthy of the angler's steel.

Of all the fresh-water fish, I consider a chalk stream trout the most lovely, as long as he is not a cannibal. Of the coarse fish I consider the tench the most attractive.

These latter vary enormously in some waters. I have seen tench of a deep green colour, others of a very dark bronze, and the tench of Thorney Pond, which do not as a rule run to a great size, are bronze on the back and sides while the belly and throat are suffused with a wonderful golden hue which quickly fades after death. Of all the coarse fish, if we do not count the eel, the pike is the ugliest – but in actual fact I know of no fish that swims which is really ugly, unless it is a very old mirror carp.

The perch would be handsome if his head were smaller, but I never like a fish with spines. The spines of a perch can inflict a very nasty wound which frequently turns septic. It is difficult to say why the perch is so armed. They do not protect it from a hungry pike, as I have frequently caught the latter when live-baiting with perch.

I have a great liking for the shape of a bream, but his slime is horrible. He is as glutinous as an eel. I get occasional eels in Thorney Pond, but I am glad to say that they are few and far between. Eels are frequently found in carp waters, probably because both carp and eels are lovers of mud.

The big eels attack and eat fish and are frequently caught when live-baiting for pike, but I doubt if they often catch a fish which is in fit condition. The eel is a useful scavenger, and this is perhaps his only good point; unless you count his excellent flavour on the table.

CHAPTER XV

IN GOD'S GOOD TIME

The very early days of spring have an especial charm for me. I mean those days which we get in February, usually one or two towards the end of the month, when, by certain hedgerow banks, one detects a faint pleasing scent of warmed grass and leaves, and where soon the prim-rolled violet leaves first show. I refer to those windless mornings when, for the first time since Christmas, the sun shines pale but warm on southern slopes, and the gentle grass snake stirs deep in his winter retreat under the earth.

This first sensation is so delicate and fleeting that one wonders if it can really be true, that soon the grey cold days will be but a memory, that these purple, naked thorns will be clothed with so dense a green garment that the eye cannot penetrate them.

The trodden track that leads across the meadow to the gate among the trees is still saturated with moisture; the foot slips on the mud. The grass shows no sign of new growth, it appears dead and flattened as though the winter had bitten deep into the roots, as though it will never rise up again. Yet in a short three months the buttercups, the clover, and the red sorrel will reach to the knees. How hard it is to believe this!

As I lift the latch of the gate, I find myself (with foolish optimism) listening for the first chiffchaff, the very first bird of spring that I hear in my little wood. The green woodpecker's laughing cry rings out, and I am glad because I know that one bird, at least, has survived the dread winter. It was shocking how my loved birds suffered during that dread time of 1947. I used to see the Little Owls sitting hunched upon the snow, so feeble that one could pick them up. The partridges hunted the stackyards, and at night crept about the hedges, where the great drifts were six and seven feet deep. Foxes waxed fat....

The spring of 1947 was a silent spring; not one green woodpecker cheered me with his wild woodland voice, and few thrushes and blackbirds sang. How starved I was for the sun, how thankful I was when it came at last to make amends! I do not suppose I shall ever see another as severe.

The fish did not suffer. When the sun shone once more, I saw them basking in their favourite haunts, though for nine weary weeks they had been roofed in with unyielding ice.

Every twenty-fifth of March I make a pilgrimage to the Pond and Wood to greet the chiffchaff. Most years he is there waiting for me, having arrived in the night.

Usually I first hear him singing among the willows. It is a faint little song, rather like his late summer song, almost a sad echo of it. I see his trim little yellow form hopping delicately among the silver buds – he seems to like to reassure himself that spring is on the way by looking at them.

Ten days later (though not always so surely) the willow warblers arrive, and their gentle falling song is even more delightful.

I walk along the winding paths among the bare thorns, noting the old nests of bullfinch, blackbird, and thrush, still firmly fixed among the spined thickets, battered, flattened, tilted, awry. The berries in them, stored by the mice, have long since gone, but those nests will remain until the leaves hide them. Most birds, even the bullfinch, build well and true.

The rooks, whose black twig bundles in the elm crowns have withstood the worst winter gales, are busy and vociferous during these fleeting sunny hours. Already I heard a new note in their voices, reminding me of boyhood days and the Easter holidays.

Dead leaves are around the hut, drifted against the wooden walls. I turn the key and go inside. I have not been within since autumn days. I recall that night in mid-September when a band of swallows came at dusk and roosted in the willows; how on three successive nights they came and I shone the torch upon their sleeping forms. I think of the night (my last night) when I slept in the hut, when the wind was blustering and cold, rattling the door and rustling among the leaves, and how I heard a faint knocking on the window. I went out with the torch and saw a single swallow huddled against the pane. The willows were deserted, his companions had gone south that day, and he was evidently the last remaining bird of the brood, probably one of the last hatch. I recall how I brought him in and warmed him in my hands and felt his diminutive fluttering heart-beats against my right thumb – I wondered if that little pumping-engine would be equal to carrying him over the high Alps.

He slept the night in the hut, on top of a bookcase over my bed, and in the morning I let him go and saw him fly over the wood. That autumn I never saw another swallow.

Above the door is a butterfly fast asleep, a peacock. It is not deceived by the sun outside; it knows that the time is not yet whan it may stir and open its wings and bask in the sun. There are other frosty nights to come, and snow, and cutting winds.

It will sleep on for another five weeks yet, and then one day, possibly at the end of March or early April, I shall gently take him and let him go out into the wood, though his life will not be long.

The 'Tortoise' stove in the corner is as I left it that September night, with the grey ashes of the long dead fire still within. Leaves have blown in under the door; they lie under the naked wooden bed. The place feels cold and damp.

I go outside and lock the door behind me. Soon I shall be here again, with my rods and blankets, my cooking pots and pans.

Down by the bank the badgers have been stirring: there are fresh pug marks on the clay. They, at any rate, have felt the quickening of spring; deep down in their ancient sett under the roots of the oak they hearken to the drums of life.

Perhaps on mild moist nights of midwinter they have come around the hut, optimistically looking for the garbage-bucket, grunting to one another in the moon's light.

The Pond seems very clear, clearer now than at any time since autumn. I can see the leaves upon the sloping floor. No weeds show, the water-lilies are invisible; the Pond appears cold and empty, there are no signs of carp. Not even a roach is to be seen, though at the willow end the sun shines full upon the pool, and gnats dance under the boughs of the oak.

How naked appears my little wood: not a bud, not a leaf visible! Between the stems I can see the dun fields and the sheep feeding. Then a lamb bleats and I catch a glimpse of it through the trees. It has its little black face towards me – which, the country people say, is a good omen for the coming year.

In a short while now, a very short while, those black bare trees will be a wall of impenetrable green, and somewhere out of sight the turtle doves will be crooning. The slow sure wheel of the seasons is such a comforting thing, so methodical, almost mechanical, but one never senses this. Each spring is a new spring and the leaves seem to be unfolding for the first time from twigs which have always been naked and black.

Each season a large family is born and grows to maturity in my little wood and pond: insects, birds, fish, animals, and plants. The badgers will have young, the fox cubs will play round the dark cavern of the earth. At least twenty woodpigeons will be born, and more than half that number will fly and go out into the world. Twenty odd blackcaps will be hatched. Eight bullfinches will build and lay, but only eight or more of the young will leave the nest. These shy and lovely rosebud finches suffer much from enemies who climb the thorns and rape the nest of eggs and young.

Thirty or more blackbirds, about the same number of thrushes, will hatch and fly safely. All these are only a tithe of the various creatures which find annual sanctuary by Thorney Pond. And yet I think, as I stand in the sun by the water side, how strange it is that all these warm, pulsing creatures are as yet out of the scheme of things, or rather, that they are impatiently awaiting life as the sleeping peacock butterfly awaits the sun.

I cannot compute the numbers of froglings which will eventually crawl laboriously away from Thorney Pond on the big Adventure, nor the millions of insects which will hatch and enjoy their brief hour.

Down in the mud at the bottom of the pond the big carp move and stir, revolving in their dull cold brains the magic of awakening summer.

Some are no doubt destined to feel the prick of a hook, and will fight a gallant battle, but the ponderous twenty-pounders (which I like to think are down there out of sight), they will no doubt have an uneventful summer. I wish them plenty of fat grubs and a good season for ground-bait – with all my heart I do.

But the sun has gone at last, a wind stirs among the oak tops, ruffling the skin of clear cold water. We are all of us waiting, waiting, and the sun and season is in no hurry. It is time to look over my rods, to look to my lines and reels. There is time yet to read a good book, to enjoy the warmth of friendship and a log fire.

We are all of us waiting, and I, being an angler, am used to waiting. The peacock butterfly, the tight-closed buds, the roots of the meadow grasses, all are awaiting God's good time. The chiffchaff, which I shall so surely hear, is at this moment no doubt hopping in an orange-grove in the sun of Spain, the gentle turtle doves are busy in an African jungle. But soon there will come to them uneasy restless thoughts, and perhaps – who knows? – into their diminutive craniums, so delicately wrought, will steal a vision of a little green wood, set in a pleasant meadow, a still dark pool, where fish lie basking, the very place where they themselves first entered into this lovely life, and where sometimes an idle man sits and fishes and gives thanks to God.